An Introduction to English S

Edinburgh Textbooks on the English Language

General Editor
Heinz Giegerich, Professor of English Linguistics (University of Edinburgh)

Editorial Board
Laurie Bauer (University of Wellington)
Derek Britton (University of Edinburgh)
Olga Fischer (University of Amsterdam)
Norman Macleod (University of Edinburgh)
Donka Minkova (UCLA)
Katie Wales (University of Leeds)
Anthony Warner (University of York)

TITLES IN THE SERIES INCLUDE

An Introduction to English Syntax
Jim Miller

An Introduction to English Phonology
April McMahon

An Introduction to English Morphology
Andrew Carstairs-McCarthy

An Introduction to English Syntax

Jim Miller

Edinburgh University Press

Edinburgh University Press Ltd
22 George Square, Edinburgh

Typeset in Janson
by Norman Tilley Graphics and
printed and bound in Great Britain
by MPG Books Ltd, Bodmin, Cornwall

A CIP Record for this book is available from the British Library

ISBN 0 7486 1254 8 (hardback)
ISBN 0 7486 1253 X (paperback)

Contents

Acknowledgements

Anthony Warner read the first draft of this book and offered many valuable comments which have helped me to improve both the organisation of the contents and the explanation of particular points. Jenny Fuchs, although busy with her studies on the second year of the Honours MA in English Language at the University of Edinburgh, gave both a student's reaction and comments worthy of professional linguists.

Derek Britton spent a considerable time devising Old English examples. Karin Søde-Woodhead drew my attention to a number of inadequacies. Will Lamb reassured me that the text was at the right level and on the right lines for an introduction to syntax. Over the past ten years, a number of classes have acted as guinea pigs for Chapters 6 and 7 on clauses and for Chapters 12 and 13 on grammar and semantics. I thank all the above and declare that I alone am responsible for any imperfections in the book.

To colleagues

This book is an introduction to syntax for students embarking on English Language courses. It might also prove useful to students taking the English Language A-level or its equivalent and to students taking university courses in Linguistics. The book does not even sketch the major syntactic constructions of English. Most of the examples are indeed from English, but the book deals with the general concepts necessary for analysing syntax (whether of English or of some other language).

Many students in the UK and elsewhere take courses in English Language and in Linguistics in their first and/or second years but then specialise in another subject. The content of this book reflects the view that such students should be taught concepts and methods that find an application in other university disciplines or outside university. This criterion excludes detailed discussion of constituent structure, tree diagrams and formal models of syntax, because these find no application outside the classroom except in computational linguistics. But even in that field, the central topics include basic clause analysis, discourse organisation, tense, aspect and modality. The concepts of head and modifier, and of subcategorisation and valency, find some application, say in the teaching of foreign languages. Also useful and applicable is knowledge of different types of clause and their function in sentences, word classes, case, transitivity and gender.

The topics mentioned in the preceding paragraph are traditional but have been greatly developed over the past thirty years; new perspectives, new data and new insights are available. More importantly, they all find applications in teaching, in speech pathology, in university courses on discourse analysis and stylistics, in courses on psycholinguistics and in cognitive science, and in the preparation of commercial and technical documents and in writing in general.

The above explains why the book has only one short chapter on constituent structure. (But Appendix 1 gives diagrams showing dependency analyses of various clauses, Appendix 2 provides constituent-structure diagrams of the traditional sort and Appendix 3 diagrams the relationships among various constructions.) Students who use this book and continue with English Language or Linguistics will learn in detail about constituent analysis and formal models of syntax in their second or later years. I hope that readers of this book will find it interesting (in places, at least), clear, and useful after their studies are finished.

To readers

We study syntax because it enables human beings to compose complex messages. Suppose a disgruntled worker utters the single word *idiot!* He or she might have muttered *stupid, unfeeling, ignorant idiot*, with four words combined into a phrase. The speaker might even have said *That stupid, unfeeling, ignorant idiot is the new manager!*, in which the phrase *the new manager* and the phrase *that stupid, unfeeling, ignorant idiot* are combined into a clause by means of *is*. (For a discussion of phrases and clauses, see Chapters 1, 2, 6 and 7.)

Syntax has to do with how words are put together to build phrases, with how phrases are put together to build clauses or bigger phrases, and with how clauses are put together to build sentences. In small and familiar situations, humans could communicate using single words and many gestures, particularly when dealing with other members of the same social grouping (nuclear family, extended family, clan and so on). But complex messages for complex situations or complex ideas require more than just single words; every human language has devices with which its speakers can construct phrases and clauses.

We habitually talk of human languages and their speakers; we ask questions such as 'How many speakers are there of Chinese/Arabic/ Spanish?' Nobody ever asks how many writers such-and-such a language has, but the distinction between speaking and writing is crucial and affects the study of syntax. It is therefore surprising that we cannot draw a major distinction between spoken and written language. Instead, the major distinction is between language for which very little planning time is available and language for which much more planning time is available. Much spoken language is indeed produced with little planning time, but some kinds are planned or semi-planned. A current-affairs report on radio is written but spoken aloud, while lectures in universities have at least an outline script in the form of 'headlines' projected onto a screen but require some improvisation. Many types of writing involve planning, such as essays, research papers and books, but other types of written text are typically produced quickly, such as personal letters and e-mail messages to friends or close colleagues.

Many kinds of spoken language, not just the spontaneous speech of domestic conversation or discussions in pubs, have a syntax that is very different from the syntax of formal writing. It is essential to understand that the differences exist not because spoken language is a degradation of written language but because any written language, whether English or Chinese, results from centuries of development and elaboration by a small number of users – clerics, administrators, lawyers and literary people. The process involves the development of complex syntactic constructions and complex vocabulary. In spite of the huge prestige enjoyed by written language in any literate society, spoken language is primary in several major respects. There are, or were until recently, societies with a spoken language but no written language, but no societies with only a written language; children usually learn to speak long before they learn to read and write; and the vast majority of human beings use speech far more often than writing.

The syntax of spontaneous spoken language has been 'designed' or 'developed' to suit the conditions of speech – little planning time, the possibility of transmitting information by loudness, pitch and general voice quality, and support from hand gestures, facial expressions and so on (what is known as 'non-verbal communication'). For a particular language, the syntax of spontaneous speech overlaps with the syntax of formal writing; there is a common core of constructions. For instance, *The instructions are useless* could be spoken or written. However, many constructions occur in speech but not in writing, and vice versa. *She doesn't say much – knows a lot though* is typical of speech, but typical of writing is *Although she does not say much, she knows a lot*.

The special syntax of spontaneous spoken language is not produced just by speakers with the minimum of formal education. One of the most detailed investigations of spoken syntax was carried out in Russia in the late 1960s and early 1970s. The speakers recorded on tape in all sorts of informal situations were doctors, lawyers and academics, but their speech turned out to be very different in syntax from written Russian. Moreover, their syntax had general properties which have turned up in bodies of spontaneous spoken English, French and German.

This book deals with concepts suitable for the analysis of all types of language, from spontaneous unplanned conversation to planned and edited formal writing. The one exception is the unit that we call 'sentence'. Attempts to apply this unit to spontaneous speech have not been successful; speakers disagree, sometimes spectacularly, on where sentences begin and end in recordings of spontaneous speech in their native language. The sentence appears to be a unit developed for formal writing. It is also appropriate for the analysis of planned speech where the syntax is that of writing.

People learn the syntax and vocabulary of formal writing from books and in school in a process that lasts into the early twenties for university graduates and can continue much longer. In general, the more exposure speakers have to formal schooling, the more easily and frequently they use in speech the syntax and vocabulary that are typical of formal writing. Individuals have choices, however; a highly educated individual may choose to keep to simple language in speech and writing, and individuals with a minimum of formal education but a large exposure to books may use very complex language in all situations.

The concept of a language is not straightforward. People think of themselves as, say, speakers of French or speakers of English, but they can be thought of as possessing a core of grammar and vocabulary and a greater or lesser number of other genres, possibly with special syntactic constructions but certainly with special vocabulary and fixed combinations of words; the language of literary criticism is different from the language of football reports. The syntactic concepts presented in this book apply to all types of English (or French or Chinese), and many of them apply to all languages.

Many differences among speakers come from the distinction between a standard variety and non-standard varieties. The standard variety of a given language is typically the one spoken by the group of people who possess military, political and economic power. In France, this was the group inhabiting the Île de France with Paris at its centre. In England (and later in Great Britain and the United Kingdom), it was the group inhabiting London and the surrounding area. (That last sentence simplifies a very complex historical process.)

Non-standard varieties tend to be spoken only, while standard varieties are spoken and written. Only standard varieties are used in education, in broadcasting, in government documents and in spoken communications from government; non-standard varieties are used at home, in many shops, among certain groups of workers and so on. There never has been a clear dividing line with all activities on one side of the line conducted in a standard variety and all activities on the other side being conducted in non-standard varieties. Many accounts of standard language convey a black-and-white picture, but it is false for spoken language; there are many shades of linguistic grey. Two important points have to be made with respect to standard and non-standard varieties (of English, say). Non-standard varieties have their own regular syntactic patterns, different in many respects from the patterns of the standard variety but nonetheless regular. The syntactic concepts introduced in the rest of this book are just as applicable to non-standard varieties as to the standard.

Syntax is neutral with respect to 'correct' and 'incorrect' English, French and so on. Analysts of English aim to cover as much data as possible. They collect samples of current speech and writing and note that examples such as (1) are typical of speech but also occur in writing while examples such as (2) occur mainly in formal writing. That is, they analyse and describe all the data they come across.

(1) Which club did you hit the winning putt with?
(2) With which club did you hit the winning putt?

Other observers of English assume it is their duty to recommend that only (2) be used in writing and preferably also in speaking. They do not just describe; they prescribe certain constructions and they proscribe others. They are likely to disparage (1) as 'sloppy' if not downright 'incorrect'. Careful analysts observe that these judges of usage are like the courtiers advising King Canute to stop the flow of the tide by issuing a command. Like the ebb and flow of the tide, usages of language and changes of usage cannot be controlled by the commands of writer or teacher, and objective analysts must include all the constructions of a given language.

The preceding comments are quite compatible with the view that speakers and writers can produce syntax that is confusing and even wrong. Sentences may be too long or organised with complex phrases right at the beginning, which makes them difficult to interpret. A writer, say someone learning English as a second language, who produces *I hope being admitted to Edinburgh University* has either not completed the sentence or has used an incorrect construction, that is, one that is unacceptable to many or even most normal adult speakers and writers of standard English. *I hope to be admitted ...* is what he or she should have used.

We said earlier in this introduction that humans need syntax in order to compose complex messages. Messages convey meaning, but elementary syntax books typically begin by stating forcibly one central important point: you cannot analyse syntax coherently and consistently by appealing in the first place to the meaning of words, phrases, clauses and sentences. Here, too, we waste no time but in Chapters 1–3 plunge into a discussion of the concepts required for an analysis of syntax that is not based on meaning.

That said, it would be wrong to deny all parallels between syntax and meaning. For example, the organisation of syntax is not entirely arbitrary. We will see in Chapter 2 that phrases consist of a central word called a head and other words which are said to modify the head. Heads and modifiers occur in regular patterns. In neutral clauses of English (see Chapter 3 on constructions), adjectives precede their head noun – *scary ideas* – and relative clauses follow their head noun – *the letter that she wrote.* Some languages, such as Turkish, are more regular than English, and both adjectives and relative clauses precede their head noun. Objects of different kinds (direct, indirect – see Chapter 10 on grammatical functions) follow the verb in neutral clauses.

There are regular patterns of syntax for making statements, asking different types of question and giving commands (see Chapter 3 on constructions). Words in English fall into a number of word classes – nouns, verbs, adjectives and so on. Over the past forty years, textbooks have regularly expressed doubt about the different word classes being connected with differences in meaning. While there is not a perfect match, the system of word classes is now seen to rest on a solid core of differences in meaning; these have to do with the kinds of things denoted by nouns, verbs and so on, and also with what speakers do with them. (See the discussion in Chapter 4 on word classes.)

Finally, there are strong correlations between differences in syntax and differences in meaning in one central area of English (and other languages) – the distinctions between past and present tense, between progressive and simple verbs (*was writing* vs *wrote*) and between singular and plural in nouns, between the Perfect and the Simple Past (*has written* vs *wrote*), between different moods and modalities. (Ignore these technical terms just now – they are explained in Chapter 13.) As psycholinguists have pointed out, human beings find arbitrary codes difficult to learn and use (random sequences of numbers, say). But similarities in syntax do tie in with similarities in meaning. Children are no better than adults at handling arbitrary codes; if there were no connection between grammar and meaning, they would find it difficult, if not impossible, to acquire their native language.

Language is at the centre of human societies; it plays a crucial part in the organisation of social activities, from government through the workplace to the home. These complex tasks require complex language, and that requires syntax.

1 Heads and modifiers

1.1 Heads and modifiers

Our discussion of syntax begins with two central ideas. The first is that certain relationships hold between words whereby one word, the **head**, controls the other words, the **modifiers**. A given head may have more than one modifier, and may have no modifier. The second idea is that words are grouped into **phrases** and that groupings typically bring together heads and their modifiers. In *the large dog*, the word *dog* is the head, and *the* and *large* are its modifiers. In *barked loudly*, the word *barked* is the head and *loudly* the modifier. (Criteria for recognising heads and modifiers will be given below.)

A phrase, then, is a group of interrelated words. As we will see in Chapter 2, groups of interrelated words can be moved around inside **clauses** as a single unit; here, we concentrate on the fact that in such groups we recognise various links among the words, between heads and their modifiers. This relationship of **modification** is fundamental in syntax. It will play an important role in the account of different types of clause (Chapter 6) and is crucial to discussions of word order in different languages.

How are we to understand the statement 'one word, the head, controls the other words, the modifiers'? Consider the sentences in (1)–(2), which also introduce the use of the asterisk – '*' – to mark unacceptable examples.

(1) a. Ethel was sitting at her desk.
     b. *The Ethel was sitting at her desk.
(2) a. *Accountant was sitting at her desk.
     b. The accountant was sitting at her desk.
     c. Accountants audit our finances every year.

Example (1a) is a grammatical sentence of English, but (1b) is not grammatical (at least as an example of standard English). *Ethel* is a type of noun that typically excludes words such as *the* and *a*. (Nouns are

1

described in Chapter 4 on word classes. Here, we will use nouns that accord with their traditional definition as words that denote people, places and things.) *Accountant* is a different type of noun; if it is singular, as in (2a), it requires a word such as *the* or *a*. In (2c), *accountants* consists of *accountant* plus the plural suffix *-s* and denotes more than one accountant. It does not require *the*. Plural nouns, of course, exclude *a* or *an* but allow words such as *some* or *more*, as shown in (3).

(3) a. *I would like an accountants to sort out my tax return.
     b. Some accountants were quietly counting in the back office.
     c. Would more accountants make any difference to my tax bill?

Another type of noun, which includes words such as *salt, sand* and *water*, can occur without any word such as *the, a* or *some*, as in (4a, b), and can occur in the plural but only with a large change in meaning. Example (4c) can only mean that different types of salt were spread.

(4) a. The gritter spread salt.
     b. The gritter spread the salt.
     c. The gritter spread salts.

Note too that a plural noun such as *gritters* allows either *less* or *fewer*, as in (5d) and (5c), whereas *salt* requires *less* and excludes *fewer*, as in (5a) and (5b).

(5) a. This gritter spread less salt than that one.
     b. *This gritter spread fewer salt than that one.
     c. There are fewer gritters on the motorway this winter.
     d. There are less gritters on the motorway this winter.

The central property of the above examples is that *Ethel, accountant, salt* and *gritter* permit or exclude the plural suffix and permit or exclude words such as *the, a, some, less* and *fewer* – note that *Ethel* excludes *the, a, some, less* and *fewer*; *salt* in (4a) excludes *a* and *fewer*; *gritters* excludes *a*; *accountant* allows both *the* and *a*, and so on.

We have looked at phrases with nouns as the controlling word, but other types of word exercise similar control. Many adjectives such as *sad* or *big* allow words such as *very* to modify them – *very sad, very big* – but exclude words such as *more* – *sadder* is fine but *more sad* is at the very least unusual. Other adjectives, such as *wooden*, exclude *very* and *more* – *very wooden, *more wooden*. That is, *wooden* excludes *very* and *more* in its literal meaning, but note that *very* is acceptable when *wooden* has a metaphorical meaning, as in *The policeman had a very wooden expression.*

Even a preposition can be the controlling word in a group. Prepositions link nouns to nouns (*books about antiques*), adjectives to nouns (*rich in minerals*) and verbs to nouns (*aimed at the target*). Most prepositions must be followed by a group of words containing a noun, or by a noun on its own, as in *(They sat) round the table, (Claude painted) with this paint-brush, (I've bought a present) for the children.* A small number of prepositions allow another preposition between them and the noun: *In behind the wood-pile (was a hedgehog), (An owl swooped on the rabbit) from up in the beech tree. In* allows *behind* and *from* allows *up*. That is, the preposition controls what-ever word or phrase follows it. Another aspect of this control can be seen from the fact that in standard English prepositions can be followed by pronouns, but they exclude *I, he, she, we* and *they* and require *me, him, her, us* and *them*: **I've bought a present for she, I've bought a present for her.*

1.2 Heads, modifiers and meaning

The distinction between heads and modifiers has been put in terms of one word, the head, that controls the other words in a phrase, the modifiers. If we think of language as a way of conveying information – which is what every speaker does with language some of the time – we can consider the head as conveying a central piece of information and the modifiers as conveying extra information. Thus in the phrase *expen-sive books* the head word *books* indicates the very large set of things that count as books, while *expensive* indicates that the speaker is drawing attention not to the whole set but to the subset of books that are expen-sive. In the longer phrase *the expensive books*, the word *the* signals that the speaker is referring to a set of books which have already been mentioned or are otherwise obvious in a particular context.

The same narrowing-down of meaning applies to phrases containing verbs. Note first that different verbs have different powers of control. Some verbs, as in (6a), exclude a direct object (to use the traditional terminology and anticipating Chapter 8), other verbs require a direct object, as in (6b), and a third set of verbs allows a direct object but does not require one, as in (6c).

(6) a. *The White Rabbit vanished his watch / The White Rabbit vanished.
   b. Dogs chase cats / *Dogs chase.
   c. Flora cooks / Flora cooks gourmet meals.

Consider the examples *drove* and *drove a Volvo*. *Drove* indicates driving in general; *drove a Volvo* narrows down the activity to driving a particular make of car. Consider further the phrase *on the plate*. The first word, *on*, signals a relationship between some entity, say a piece of toast or a knife, and the surface of something; *the plate* tells us what that something is, that is, it narrows down the meaning 'being on' to 'being on a particular plate'.

Finally in this brief set of examples, we return to the point made earlier in passing that heads may have several modifiers. This is most easily illustrated with verbs; the phrase *bought a present for Jeanie in Jenners last Tuesday* contains four modifiers of *bought* – *a present*, *for Jeanie*, *in Jenners* and *last Tuesday*. *A present* signals what was bought and narrows down the activity from just buying to buying a present as opposed, say, to buying the weekly groceries. *For Jeanie* narrows the meaning down further – not just 'buy a present' but 'buy a present for Jeanie', and similarly for the phrases *in Jenners* and *last Tuesday*.

1.3 Complements and adjuncts

The last example, *bought a present for Jeanie in Jenners last Tuesday*, brings us to the second major distinction in this chapter. Modifiers fall into two classes – obligatory modifiers, known as complements, and optional modifiers, known as adjuncts. The distinction was first developed for the phrases that modify verbs, and indeed applies most easily to the modifiers of verbs; we will focus on verbs, but the distinction is also applied to the modifiers of nouns. Before discussing the division of modifiers into complements and adjuncts, we must take the example at the beginning of this paragraph and convert it to a complete clause, say *My mother bought a present for Jeanie in Jenners last Tuesday*. We saw from (6a–c) that the verb controls whether a direct object is excluded, required or merely allowed. (The term 'direct object' is discussed in Chapter 8.)

From these examples, we might conclude that the verb controls only the phrases that follow it; but the verb can be seen as controlling every other phrase in the clause. *(My) mother* in the revised example above is the subject of the verb. As will be demonstrated in Chapter 8, the subject of a clause plays an important role; nonetheless, in a given clause the verb controls the subject noun too. *Bought* requires a human subject noun; that is, it does in everyday language but behaves differently in the language of fairy stories, which narrate events that are unconstrained by the biological and physical laws of this world. A verb such as FLOW requires a subject noun denoting a liquid; if in a given clause it has a subject noun denoting some other kind of entity, FLOW imposes an interpretation of that entity as a liquid. (Of course, some entities can be either liquids or solids; molten steel flows, solid steel does not.) Thus people talk of a crowd flowing along a road, of traffic flowing smoothly or of ideas flowing freely. Such talk offers a view of the crowd moving along a road held in by the buildings on either side and propelled by a mysterious motive force, just as a river moves along in a mysterious fashion held in by its banks. What we are considering is the distinction between literal language and figurative or metaphorical language. The distinction will not be explored here, but it is important to be aware that many of the constraints which linguists discuss apply to literal language but dissolve in figurative language.

Returning to the clause *My mother bought a present for Jeanie in Jenners last Tuesday*, we will say that the verb *bought* controls all the other phrases in the clause and is the head of the clause. It requires a human noun to its left, here *mother*; it requires a noun to its right that denotes something concrete (although we talk figuratively of buying ideas in the sense of agreeing with them). It allows, but does not require, time expressions such as *last Tuesday* and place expressions such as *in Jenners*. Such expressions convey information about the time when some event happened and about the place where it happened. With verbs, such time and place expressions are always optional and are held to be adjuncts. The major exception is BE, which has its own syntactic patterns. Phrases that are obligatory are called complements. (The term 'complement' derives from a Latin verb 'to fill'; the idea conveyed by 'complement' is that a complement expression fills out the verb (or noun and so on), filling it out or completing it with respect to syntax but also with respect to meaning. The term 'adjunct' derives from the Latin verb 'join' or 'add' and simply means 'something adjoined', tacked on and not part of the essential structure of clauses.) All verbs in English declarative clauses require a noun to their left; even where the buyers are known, they must be mentioned by means of a noun. Verbs such as BUY also require a noun to their right. Without one, the clause in which they occur is incomplete and the message conveyed by the clause is incomplete for speakers of English.

1.4 Clauses

The technical term 'clause' has slipped into the discussion without being explained. Suppose we want to describe different paperweights. To distinguish them, we talk of their shape, height, weight and colour and the material from which they are made. Shape, height and so on are the basic units we use to describe the paperweights, but we might need other units that enable us to talk about height (inches, centimetres), weight (ounces and grammes) and colour (blue, green). In order to talk about syntax coherently, we need units for our analysis. One unit is the phrase, which enables us to describe the relationship between other units, namely heads and modifiers, as in *the accountant, very unhappy* and *in behind the sofa*.

Another unit is the clause, which enables us to talk coherently about the relationships between verbs and different types of phrase. An ideal clause contains a phrase referring to an action or state, a phrase or phrases referring to the people and things involved in the action or state, and possibly phrases referring to place and time. *My mother bought a present* is a clause. The phrase *my mother* refers to the buyer, *bought* refers to the action and *a present* refers to what was bought. We can add the phrase *for Jeanie*, which refers to the person benefiting from the action. Finally, we can tack on, or leave out, the place phrase *in Jenners* and the time phrase *last Tuesday*.

The clause is a unit which as a minimum consists of a verb and its complements but which may consist of a verb, its complements and its adjuncts. The clause is a useful unit because it gives us a framework for discussing the relationship between, for example, *bought* and the other phrases. We will see later that it also gives a framework for talking coherently about constituent structure (Chapter 2), syntactic linkage (Chapter 9) and statements, questions and commands (Chapter 6).

Note that in the last paragraph but one, one of the phrases that turned out to be adjuncts contains a preposition, *in*, while the other one consists of an adjective, *last*, and a noun, *Tuesday*. (Nouns and prepositions and the general concept of word classes will be discussed in Chapter 4.) The example of the excursion to Jenners conveniently illustrates the lack of a reliable correlation between the type of a given phrase (does it have a preposition, noun or adjective as its head?) and the phrase's function as complement or adjunct. Consider (7).

(7) The cat shot into the kitchen on Sunday morning carrying a dead
     mouse.

As in the Jenners example, the time expression *on Sunday morning* signals the time when the event happened. Like the phrase *carrying a dead mouse*, it is optional. Consider now the phrase *into the kitchen* and its relationship to *shot*. This phrase is obligatory with this particular verb. *The cat shot is not acceptable, whereas *The cat shot off* or *The cat shot into the kitchen* are correct. That is, the phrase *into the kitchen* is obligatory and therefore a complement of *shot*. It expresses direction, where the cat moved to, and directional phrases in general are complements. We must note, however, that directional phrases are not always obligatory. Consider (8).

(8) The cat pranced into the kitchen carrying a dead mouse.

If the phrases *into the kitchen* and *carrying a dead mouse* are excised, what is left is still an acceptable sentence, *The cat pranced*. Nonetheless, the directional phrase *into the kitchen* is treated as a complement. The reason is that the occurrence of directional phrases is closely bound up with the meaning of verbs; verbs expressing movement allow or require them. Verbs that do not express movement exclude them, as in *The cat lies onto the rug in front of the fire* vs *The cat lies on the rug in front of the fire*. In contrast, phrases expressing the place where something happened occur with all sorts of verbs, whether or not they express movement.

At this point, we anticipate Chapter 5, 'The lexicon', and describe the state of affairs in terms of what goes into the dictionary entries of verbs; if it has to be stated in the dictionary whether a given verb or subset of verbs excludes (or requires) a particular type of phrase, that phrase is a complement. The dictionary entry for *lie* must state that it excludes directional phrases, whereas the entry for *shoot* (at least in the meaning it has in (7)) must state that *shoot* requires a directional phrase. The dictionary entry for *prance* will state that the verb allows a directional phrase but does not require one.

1.5 Dictionary entries and collocations

An important point implicit in the preceding paragraph is that the status of phrases as complement or adjunct varies from verb to verb. This point is worth emphasising here because it is part of the larger question of the relationship between grammar and dictionary that will be discussed in Chapter 5. It also introduces a third property of complements. English possesses (as do other languages) combinations of verb and object in which the actual lexical items that can occur are severely limited. In English (at least in the UK) you can *toast bread*, *toast marshmallows* or even *toast your toes*. You do not *grill bread*, in spite of the fact that the processes of toasting and grilling are similar (if you choose not to use the toaster). Similarly, we talk of braising meat (but not usually other items of food). Other areas than cooking offer examples of particular verbs typically combining with particular nouns; people lay tables, chop or split logs and kindling (even in these days of almost ubiquitous central heating), make beds and vire money or funds (if you are a civil servant or university administrator).

These regular fixed combinations of verbs and nouns are called collocations, and they involve heads and complements. Fixed combinations of verb and adjective are also found – *prove useless*, *prove necessary* – and a good number of verbs require particular prepositions. *Blame someone for something* and *blame something on someone* are set expressions in which only the prepositions *for* or *on* can occur; this is information that must be stated in the dictionary entry for *blame*. It must be made clear that these collocations are not proposed as a criterion for recognising complements. The central criteria are whether or not a particular phrase is obligatory with a particular verb, as with *shot* and *into the kitchen* in (7), or whether a particular type of phrase has to be mentioned in the dictionary entry for a particular verb. The collocational facts constitute interesting extra information but, and this is the difficulty, are not confined to verbs and their complement nouns; they apply to adjectives and nouns – *heavy smoker, heavy drinker, staple diet, staple crop, staple industry* – and to combinations of adjective and another word, for example, *brand new, wide awake, rock solid, frozen hard*. On the main criterion for complements, being obligatory, *brand, wide, rock* and *hard* are not complements of *new, awake, solid* and *frozen*, which is why collocations are not a test for complement status but merely an additional set of interesting facts.

1.6 Verbs, complements and the order of phrases

This chapter finishes with one more technical term and one last fact about heads and complements. The relationships between heads and modifiers are called dependencies or dependency relations. In this chapter, heads have been described as controlling modifiers; modifiers are said to depend on, or to be dependent on, their heads. Heads and their modifiers typically cluster together to form a phrase, certainly in formal written language. In accordance with a long tradition in Europe, verbs are treated here as the head, not just of phrases, but of whole clauses. (This idea is discussed further in Chapter 9.) In clauses, the verb and its complements tend to occur close together, with the adjuncts pushed towards the outside of the clause, as shown by the examples in (9). (Remember that the subject noun is regarded as a complement, since it is obligatory.)

(9) a. Maisie drove her car from Morningside to Leith on Wednesday.
     b. On Wednesday Maisie drove her car from Morningside to Leith.
     c. Maisie drove her car on Wednesday from Morningside to Leith.

In (9a), the object *her car* is next to the verb, followed by the directional phrases *from Morningside* and *to Leith*. As discussed above, objects and directional phrases are complements. The time-when phrase *on Wednesday* is at the end of the clause in (9a) and at the beginning of the clause in (9b). In (9b), it is closer to *drove*, but this is not important. What is important is the fact that the adjunct does not come between the head and any of the complements. This does happen in (9c), where *on Wednesday* separates the complement *her car* from the other complement *to Leith*. Example (9c) is at the least awkward – although there might be contexts in which that order of phrases would be appropriate.

Summary

Every phrase contains a head and possibly, but not necessarily, one or more modifiers. Each clause has a head, the verb. There are two types of modifiers, namely complements and adjuncts. Adjuncts are optional; complements are typically obligatory and are always mentioned in the lexical entries for verbs (or nouns or prepositions). Many collocation restrictions apply to heads and complements (but also to phrases other than complements). Heads and complements are typically adjacent; where a head has two or more complements, adjuncts typically come before or after the sequence of head and complements.

Exercises

1. Consider the modifiers of the verbs in the following sentences. (For the purposes of this exercise, exclude the grammatical subjects.) Which of the modifiers are obligatory and which are optional? Which of the modifiers are complements and which are adjuncts?

1. Sir Thomas agreed with Edmund.
2. Mr Elton delivered a charade to Emma for a friend.
3. She thrust the documents into her briefcase.
4. Raskolnikov killed the old woman with an axe.
5. Mr D'Arcy met the Gardiners at Pemberley in the summer.
6. Frank sent a piano to Jane Fairfax.
7. The porter placed the letter on the secretary's desk.
8. Harriet imagined that Mr Elton would propose to her.
9. The picnic was held at Box Hill in the summer.
   [Treat *was held* as a single verb.]
10. He executed great vengeance upon them with furious rebukes.
11. We were expecting the worst that day in 1968.
12. The report details the proposals for the chief executive.

2. Pick out four examples of heads and modifiers in each of the following sentences (which are from William Dalrymple's book *From the Holy Mountain* (Flamingo, 1998). You will notice that modifiers may themselves contain heads. Thus in the phrase *sitting at her desk* the head *sitting* is modified by *at her desk*. The phrase *at her desk* has as its head the word *at*, which has as its modifier the phrase *her desk*. The head of the latter phrase is *desk*, which has *her* as its modifier.

1. I ate breakfast in a vast Viennese ballroom with a sprung wooden floor and dadoes dripping with recently reapplied gilt.

2. The lift is a giant baroque birdcage, entered through a rainforest of potted palms.
3. On the wall nearby, newly dusted, is a framed diploma from the 1932 Ideal Homes Exhibition, signed by the mayor of East Ham.

2 Constituent structure

2.1 Heads, modifiers and arrangements of words

In Chapter 1, we discussed the relations between heads and modifiers and at the end of the chapter labelled these relations 'dependencies'. Dependencies are central to syntax. To make sense of a clause or sentence in written language or of a series of clauses in spontaneous speech, we have to pick out each head and the words that modify it. This task is made easier by the organisation of words into phrases and clauses. Speakers and writers produce words and phrases one after the other. (It does not matter whether the writer sets out words from left to right, as in English texts, or right to left, as in Arabic texts.) Heads and modifiers tend to occur next to each other. For instance, in English, nouns can be modified by various types of words and phrases – adjectives, prepositional phrases and relative clauses, not to mention words such as *a*, *the*, *this* and *some*. Examples are given in (1).

(1) a. the house
    b. the splendid house
    c. the house on the hilltop
    d. the house which they built out of reinforced concrete

In (1a), *house* is modified by the definite article *the*; in (1b) it is modified by the definite article and by the adjective *splendid*. The definite article, the indefinite article *a* and demonstratives such as *this* and *that* precede their head noun, but certain modifiers follow their head noun. Examples are the prepositional phrase *on the hilltop* in (1c) and the relative clause *which they built out of reinforced concrete* in (1d).

In noun phrases in some other languages, the order of head and modifiers follows a stricter pattern, with all modifiers either preceding or following the head. In French, for example, most adjectives and all prepositional phrases and relative clauses follow the noun, although the definite and indefinite articles precede it. This is demonstrated in (2).

11

(2) a. la   maison
       the house

   b. la   maison splendide
      the house splendid   'the splendid house'

   c. la   maison sur   la   colline
      the house on   the hill   'the house on the hill'

   d. la   maison qu' ils   ont construite en béton   armé
      the house which they have built   of concrete reinforced
      'the house which they built of reinforced concrete'

The adjective *splendide*, the prepositional phrase *sur la colline* and the relative clause *qu'ils ont construite en béton armé* all follow the head noun. At this point, we come up against one of the interesting (or annoying) facts of French and indeed of all human languages: most patterns have exceptions. In French, a small number of adjectives precede their head noun, as in *une jolie ville* (a pretty town) and *un jeune étudiant* (a young student), but the large majority of adjectives follow their head noun.

Returning to English, we see that in certain declarative clauses the modifiers of prepositions follow their head preposition. Example (3a) shows the typical pattern, with the preposition *into* followed by *the kitchen*; (3b) shows an impossible example, with *into* at the beginning of the clause and *the kitchen* at the end; and (3c) shows the correct structure.

(3) a. Jeeves shimmered into the room.
    b. *Into Jeeves shimmered the room.
    c. Into the room shimmered Jeeves.

In some other English clauses, the noun-phrase modifier of a preposition can be separated from its head preposition. Example (4a) is the typical way of questioning *room* in (3a). In it, *which room* is at the front of the clause, and *into* is 'stranded' at the end of the clause. Example (4b) is also acceptable but is mainly used in formal writing.

(4) a. Which room did Jeeves shimmer into?
    b. Into which room did Jeeves shimmer?

We can note in passing that similar stranding is found in clauses introduced by *which* or *who*. In formal writing, a preposition plus *which/who* turns up at the front of the clause, as in *the room into which Jeeves shimmered*. In informal writing and in informal speech, the preposition is left behind at the end of the clause, as in *the room which Jeeves shimmered into*.

Verbs can be modified by a number of items, as we have seen in

Chapter 1. Example (5) shows the order of modifiers in a neutral clause, that is, a clause in which no particular word or phrase is emphasised.

(5) Barbara handed the results to Alan on Tuesday.

Barbara, the subject noun phrase, precedes the verb, but the other modifiers follow it – the noun phrase (direct object) *the results*, the prepositional phrase (oblique object) *to Alan* and the prepositional phrase (adverb of time) *on Tuesday*. (The concepts 'subject', 'direct object' and 'oblique object' are discussed in Chapter 8.) Typically, the subject and the direct object are immediately next to the verb, the subject preceding it, the direct object following it. In (5), the subject *Barbara* and the direct object *the results* are next to the verb. In other languages, the verbs and modifiers are arranged in patterns that put all the modifiers either before or after the verb. In written Turkish, for instance, the order in neutral clauses is that the verb comes last, preceded by all the modifiers.

2.2 Tests for phrases

The arrangement of words into phrases and phrases into clauses may seem self-evident from the above discussion, particularly if you are a native speaker of English or a non-native speaker who knows English well. In fact, it is not always clear how the words in a given phrase are arranged or how the phrases are arranged in a given clause. Fortunately, tests have been developed to help analysts.

2.2.1 Transposition

Many sequences of words can be moved together into different slots in a clause; this is evidence that the words form a phrase. Let us go back to (3a), *Jeeves shimmered into the room*. We can think of (3a) as being converted to (3c) by the words *into the room* being moved, or transposed, to the front of the clause. This transposition indicates that the three separate words combine into a larger block, a phrase. Transposition also applies to phrases without prepositions. The words *the results* in (5) can be moved to the front of the clause to give *The results Barbara handed to Alan on Tuesday*, a clause that is appropriate if the speaker or writer continues, for example, *The actual scripts she kept until Friday*.

The above examples of transposition have to do with a sequence of words being moved from one position in a clause to another position without any other changes in the clause. (Remember the comment from Chapter 1 that the clause is a unit of analysis within which we can talk coherently about the order of phrases and the fact that phrases can occupy different positions.) Transposition is one of the tests that reveal whether a given sequence of words make up a phrase or are just words that happen to come one after the other. If you know English well, you may be tempted to think that such a test is unnecessary; but two facts speak against this temptation. One is that in spite of the vast amount of research on English syntax in the twentieth century we still come across examples whose structure is not obvious. The second fact is that many linguists work not just on languages other than English but on languages which have been little studied or not studied at all. In these circumstances, tests such as transposition are essential.

The test of transposition is also applied in a slightly different fashion. Consider the active clause in (6a) and the passive clause in (6b).

(6) a. The pupils in this maths class gave cakes to Margaret every Friday.
     b. Cakes were given to Margaret every Friday by the pupils in this maths class.

The phrase *the pupils in this maths class* is at the beginning of the clause in (6a) and refers to the people doing the giving. The same sequence is at the end of the clause in (6b) and is the complement of the preposition *by*. In contrast with (3a) and (3b), the differences between (6a) and (6b) consist of more than just a group of words being moved from one position to another. Example (6a) contains *gave*, while (6b) contains the words *were* and *given*. Example (6b) also contains the prepositional phrase *by the pupils in this maths class*, whereas (6a) has no prepositional phrase. When we use 'transposition' with respect to examples such as (6a) and (6b), we are talking about sequences of words that turn up in a particular order in one position in one construction and about the same sequences of words turning up in the same order in another construction. The sequence *the pupils in this maths class* occurs in the different constructions in (6a) and (6b). (Constructions are discussed in Chapter 3.)

The test of transposition applies to other sequences of words, as shown by (7).

(7) a. This parcel is *very heavy*.
     b. This *very heavy* parcel was delivered yesterday.
     c. *Very heavy*, this parcel!
     d. What this parcel is is *very heavy*.

In (7a), the sequence of words/the phrase *very heavy* is the complement of *is*; in (7b) it is the modifier of *parcel*. It turns up at the beginning of the spoken construction in (7c). In (7d) it is also the complement of *is*, but in a special emphatic construction. *Very* can be replaced by words such as *astonishingly*, and the sequence can be made longer – *astonishingly and frighteningly heavy* – but can still be transposed, as shown in *This parcel is astonishingly and frighteningly heavy, this astonishingly and frighteningly heavy parcel was delivered yesterday, What this parcel is is astonishingly and frighteningly heavy*.

Examples (3a) and (3c) show that a sequence of words introduced by a preposition – *into the room* – can be transposed. Another example is given in (8).

(8) a. We felled the laburnum *with this chainsaw*.
     b. *With this chainsaw* we felled the laburnum.

2.2.2 Substitution

The essential idea behind this test is that a single word can substitute for a number of words hanging together as a phrase. This is demonstrated in (9).

(9) a. Barbara handed *the intriguing results of the latest examination* to Alan on Tuesday.
     b. Barbara handed *them* to Alan on Tuesday.

Them in (9b) substitutes for *the intriguing results of the latest examination* in (9a). Similarly, in (6a) and (6b) *David* can be substituted for *the pupils in this maths class*: *David baked cakes for Margaret every Friday* and *Cakes were baked for Margaret every Friday by David*.

The test of substitution applies to sequences of words with adjectives, such as those in (7); *This parcel is very heavy, This parcel is astonishingly and frighteningly heavy* or simply *This parcel is heavy*. The single adjective *heavy* substitutes for the sequences *very heavy* and *astonishingly and frighteningly heavy* but another type of substitution is possible, using the specialised substitution word *so*. Consider the dialogue in (10). (Here capital letters represent different speakers.)

(10) A. This large parcel is *very heavy*.
      B. No it's not.
      C. It is *so*.

The test of *so*-substitution exemplified in (10) is straightforward in that the sequence *very heavy* is removed and *so* is dropped into the empty slot. Another type of *so*-substitution is rather indirect. Consider (11).

(11) This large parcel is *very heavy* and *so* is this small packet.

There is no doubt that *so* 'stands for' *very heavy*. The reason for calling this substitution 'indirect' is that *so* has not simply been dropped into the slot occupied by *very heavy* but has been moved to the front of the clause. Nonetheless, *so*-substitution is a good indication that sequences such as *very heavy* form a larger unit.

Substitution can be applied to sequences introduced by prepositions, as in (12) and (13).

(12) a. Vera is crocheting in the lounge.
     b. Vera is crocheting there.
(13) a. Grandma is coming to Mr Chalky's school tomorrow.
     b. Grandma is coming here tomorrow.

There in (12b) substitutes for *in the lounge* in (12a), and *here* in (13b) substitutes for *to Mr Chalky's school* in (13a). Examples in which a single preposition substitutes for a whole sequence are difficult to find. This is mainly because prepositions typically require a complement, but also because in standard written English there is a contrast between *in* for location and *into* for movement, and for many speakers there is a contrast between *out of* for movement and *out* for location, as in (14).

(14) a. The cat was sleeping in the kitchen.
     b. The cat trotted into the kitchen.
     c. The mouse jumped out of the cheese-box.
     d. The mouse was out the cheese-box.

In informal spoken English, and certainly in non-standard varieties of English, *in* and *out* express both location and movement, and (14b, c) can be expressed as (15a, b).

(15) a. The cat trotted in the kitchen.
     b. The mouse jumped out the cheese-box.

These examples can be shortened to those in (16).

(16) a. The cat trotted in.
     b. The mouse jumped out.

In these examples, *in* and *out* can be treated as single words substituting for the longer phrases *in the kitchen* and *out the cheese-box*. However, for the large majority of prepositions, the substitution of a preposition for preposition plus noun phrase does not work, whether in writing or informal speech, in standard or non-standard English.

Finally in this section, let us note that all the above examples show a sequence of words being replaced by one word. The converse is that a single word can be replaced by a sequence of words: *Cheese is good* can be changed to *That French cheese with the blue veins is good*. The latter example is occasionally described in terms of *cheese* being expanded to *that French cheese with the blue veins*, but it is treated here as a type of substitution.

2.2.3 Ellipsis

Consider the examples in (17).

(17) a. The terrier attacked the burglar. The terrier savaged the burglar's ankles.
   b. *The terrier* attacked the burglar and *the terrier* savaged the burglar's ankles.
   c. The terrier attacked the burglar and [   ] savaged the burglar's ankles.

Example (17a) contains two separate clauses. In (17b), the clauses are conjoined by *and*; this gives a single sentence consisting of two clauses, each beginning with *the terrier*. (See Chapter 6 for a discussion of clauses and sentences.) Example (17c) is produced by deleting the second occurrence of *the terrier*. The square brackets in (17c) mark the site of the missing words, which are said to have been ellipted. Example (17c) is an example of ellipsis. The important point about this type of ellipsis is that it applies only to complete phrases. Sentences such as *The fierce terrier attacked the burglar and terrier savaged the burglar's ankles* are incorrect, because *terrier* must be preceded by *the*. Example (17b) is peculiar because speakers and writers of English do not repeat phrases in this manner but either ellipt the second occurrence of the phrase as in (17c) or use a substitute such as *he, she* or *it*. *The burglar* occurs twice, once as the phrase at the beginning of (17b) and again in the bigger phrase *the burglar's ankles*. In the latter phrase *the burglar*, or rather *the burglar* plus the possessive suffix *'s*, is replaced by *his*: *The terrier attacked the burglar and she savaged his ankles*.

2.3 Phrases: words and slots

At this point in the discussion, we need to comment on the concept of phrase. In everyday usage, the term 'phrase' is applied only to sequences of more than one word. This is easily demonstrated with (5), reproduced below as (18a) and (18b).

(18) a. Barbara handed the results to Alan on Tuesday.
   b. Barbara handed them to Alan on Tuesday.

Examples (18a) and (18b) both contain the phrases (in the everyday sense) *to Alan* and *on Tuesday*. In contrast, *Barbara* in (18a) and *them* in

(18b) do not constitute everyday phrases because they each consist of just one word. In syntactic analysis, a distinction between 'phrase' and 'word' is observed, but it does not match the everyday distinction since both *Barbara* and *them* are treated as phrases. What is meant by 'phrase' is a slot in which one or more words can occur, or indeed in which other phrases can occur. In (18b) the phrase *them* consists of only one word, but the term 'phrase' is used because what is being said is 'Here is a slot in which it is possible for more than one word to occur'. The fact that there is only one word in the slot in this particular example is just an accident; *them* can be replaced by a longer sequence, say *the results of the maths examination sat just before Christmas.*

In both (18a) and (18b), the first phrase consists of a single word, *Barbara*, but this too is an accident of these examples. *Barbara* could be replaced by *Margaret's hard-working colleague*. Likewise, the phrase *to Alan* contains a noun phrase, *Alan* – just one word, but it could be replaced by *her colleague who was collating the examination marks*. And in the phrase *on Tuesday*, a longer sequence could be substituted for *Tuesday*, such as *the day he forgot his coat and got absolutely drenched*.

The above discussion brings to our attention a universal and crucial ambiguity. Terms such as 'noun' and 'verb' will be discussed in Chapter 4, and in this chapter we have used terms such as 'noun phrase' and 'prepositional phrase'. These terms are applied to words; we talk of looking for such-and-such a noun in the dictionary. They are applied to sequences of words; many dictionaries contain fixed sequences such as *a rolling stone*. They are also applied, and this is where the ambiguity lies, to the slots in clauses in which particular words or phrases occur. This brings us back to the point made above that when *Barbara* is labelled a noun phrase the label captures the fact that this single word occupies a slot that could be occupied by a sequence of words, a phrase.

2.4 Coordination

Words of the same type can be coordinated, that is, joined by special words such as *and* and *or*. Phrases of the same type can be coordinated, and clauses of the same type. In this section, we focus on words and phrases. In the clause *John and his energetic wife landscaped the garden twice last year*, *John* is a phrase consisting of a single word and *his energetic wife* is a phrase consisting of three words. In spite of the disparity in length, the two phrases are coordinated – *John and his energetic wife*. In the noun phrase *the bright and incredibly sharp air over Doubtful Sound*, the one-word adjective phrase *bright* is coordinated with the two-word adjective phrase *incredibly sharp*. The fact of the coordination is one of the reasons for recognising *bright* as a phrase.

2.5 Concluding comments

We finish the discussion in this chapter with five general comments. The first is simply that the tests of transposition and substitution apply inside clauses, although they are often said to apply inside sentences. This is one reason why the clause is a useful unit for our analysis; it enables us to handle the fact that sequences of words occur in different positions and to apply the tests to sequences whose status is not clear. Ellipsis too applies inside a clause, but its operation takes two or more clauses into account, since it deletes phrases that are repeated from one clause to the following one.

The second comment concerns the different types of phrase. The labels 'noun phrase', 'prepositional phrase' and 'adjective phrase' are in general use. A phrase with a noun as its head is a noun phrase, for example, *her **colleague** who was collecting the exam scripts*; a phrase with a preposition as its head is a prepositional phrase, for example *to Alan*; a phrase with an adjective as its head is an adjective phrase, for example *exceedingly **sorry** about the mistake*. Sequences such as *quickly* and *unbelievably **quickly*** constitute adverbial phrases, that is, phrases in which the adverb – here, *quickly* – is the head. The question of verb phrases will be discussed in Chapter 10.

The third comment concerns the fact that phrases can contain other phrases. The phrase *to her colleague* in the extended version of (18a) discussed in Section 2.3 is a prepositional phrase; inside it is the noun phrase *her colleague*. The phrase *to Alan*, discussed just above, is also a prepositional phrase containing a noun phrase, which happens to consist of one word, *Alan*. The phrase *the rather intriguing results of the examination* is a noun phrase. Its head is *results*, a noun which is modified by *the*, by *rather intriguing* and by *of the examination*. *Rather intriguing* is an adjective phrase whose head is the adjective *intriguing*. This adjective is modified by *rather*. There are two more phrases inside the large noun phrase. One is the prepositional phrase *of the examination*, with the preposition *of* as its head. The other is inside the prepositional phrase and is the noun phrase *the examination*. This example, *the rather intriguing results of the examination*, is instructive; it shows how a phrase may have more than one phrase inside it – *rather intriguing*, *of the examination*, and *the examination* are all inside the noun phrase *the rather intriguing results of the examination*; it shows how a phrase can contain a phrase of the same type – the noun phrase *the examination* is inside the larger noun phrase *the rather intriguing results of the examination*.

Phrases can also contain clauses, as in the example in the paragraph following (4) *the room which Jeeves shimmered into*. This is a noun phrase with *room* as its head. *Room* is modified by the relative clause *which Jeeves shimmered into.* In *the idea that David Hume might wear a toga* the head noun *idea* is modified by the noun complement clause *that David Hume might wear a toga.* (For a discussion of relative clauses and noun complement clauses, see Chapter 6.)

These examples demonstrate an extremely important property of language, namely the ability of phrases and clauses to be indefinitely extended. Probably all English-speaking children at some point in their primary-school education discover that you can take a main clause such as *I know* and add to it the complement clause *that he knows* and then add the complement clause *that I know,* to yield *I know that he knows that I know* and so on. Not every child can produce such examples with the same skill, and comprehension usually fades after three or four complement clauses have been added.

The fourth comment has to do with the title of this chapter, 'Constituent Structure'. We have talked of words constituting phrases, and we can also talk of phrases constituting clauses. As we will see in Chapter 6, we can also talk of clauses constituting sentences. Another way of putting these ideas is to say, for example, that words are the constituents, or constituent parts, of phrases, that phrases are the constituents of bigger phrases or of clauses and that clauses are the constituents of sentences. The arrangements of words into phrases, phrases into clauses and clauses into sentences is known as constituent structure.

The final comment is that very little of the arrangement of words into phrases, phrases into bigger phrases, phrases into clauses and so on is signalled in either speech or writing. In many types of written text, writers signal how they organise clauses into sentences: they may signal boundaries between clauses by means of commas or semi-colons, and individual words are typically kept apart by a space. But there are no conventions of punctuation that point to the intricate structure of a complex noun phrase such as *the very intriguing results of the examinations.*

In speech, especially spontaneous conversation, practically nothing is signalled. In the reading-aloud of written texts, the reader may pause between sentences, but typically does not do so between clauses and certainly not between individual words; speakers very seldom utter words one at a time and with a gap between each one. Even when carefully reading a text aloud, speakers may pause at the end of sentences, clauses or phrases but not after every word. Of course, we do leave a space between words when we write, but the spaces in written texts do not correspond to spaces in speech. If you listen to someone speaking a language you do not know, whether German, Finnish or Turkish, you will have no idea where words begin and end; if you pick up a text written in one of these languages, you will see the gaps between the words and will immediately be able to ask about the meaning of particular words.

Equally, in spontaneous speech, speakers typically do not pause between clauses. When they do pause, they are just as likely to do so in the middle of clauses, in the middle of phrases or even in the middle of words, depending on rapidity of speech, emotional state, whether the speaker has just run up a flight of stairs or has been sitting quietly in an armchair, and so on. All these properties of speech point to the arrangement of words into phrases, phrases into clauses and so on as something abstract. Linguists put the arrangements, the structure, into their analysis of particular clauses, but ordinary native speakers of a given language carry knowledge of the arrangements in their heads. Faced with a line of words on the page or a sequence of sounds produced by a speaker, readers and hearers invest the sequence with structure; they 'read' into it the words, the organisation of words into phrases and so on.

Summary

Heads and their modifiers are typically grouped together inside clauses. Different languages have different orders of head and modifiers. There are three tests for whether a sequence of words forms a phrase: transposition, substitution and ellipsis. In syntax, the term 'phrase' is applied to single words and to sequences of words. This reflects the view that a single noun such as *sand* occupies a slot in which a phrase could occur. An example of a slot is ___ *is needed*; into it can go, for example, *sand*, as in *Sand is needed*, or *special sand for the lawn*, as in *Special sand for the lawn is needed*. Phrases can be extended indefinitely, different types of phrase have different types of head, phrases occur in clauses, but clauses can also occur inside phrases.

Exercises

1. The following sentences exemplify the criteria of transposition, substitution, coordination and ellipsis applied to one type of phrase. What type of phrase is it and which criteria apply to which examples?

1. I put the letter into the top drawer of the bureau.
2. I put the letter there.
3. Where I put the letter was into the top drawer of the bureau.
4. Into the top drawer of the bureau I put the letter.

5. It was into the top drawer of the bureau that I put the letter.
6. I put the letter either there or into the top drawer of the bureau.
7. I put into the top drawer of the bureau the letter, my wallet and an old watch.

2. Analyse the following examples into phrases. Label each phrase, for example as noun phrase, adverbial phrase and so on, as appropriate. If in doubt about whether words that are next to each other in an example constitute a phrase, apply the tests as demonstrated in Exercise 1 above. For example, in (1) *they* can be substituted for *the pedestrians offended by the dangerously selfish action of the driver*; *him* can be replaced by *the selfish driver*; *into the harbour* can be replace by *off*, and so on. The sequence *into the harbour* occurs in the different construction *Into the harbour they threatened to throw him*. That is, the tests of substitution and transposition indicate that *into the harbour* is a phrase, a single constituent.

1. The pedestrians offended by the dangerously selfish action of the driver threatened to throw him into the harbour.
2. To throw him into the harbour was illegal but an understandable reaction by the visitors on the quayside.
3. Brazil's tropical forests are amazingly rich in fauna and flora.
4. The person sitting at the window is my wife.
5. Sitting at the window my wife noticed that our neighbour's dog was outside.
6. Susan always drinks black coffee.
7. Susan always drinks her coffee black.
8. In his usual carefree fashion John ran up an enormous bill.
9. In his exuberance John ran up an enormous hill.

3 Constructions

3.1 Introduction

We have looked at heads and modifiers and at the organisation of smaller units into bigger units, words into phrases and phrases into bigger phrases. We now move on to look at constructions, the relatively general patterns that recur in a given language. Since words, phrases, clauses and sentences are all built out of smaller units according to particular patterns, the concept of construction is relevant to all areas of grammar. For instance, many, though clearly not all, words are built out of smaller bits; *field* consists of one stem. *Fielded*, as in *fielded the ball*, and *fielder*, as in cricket, are built from the stem plus a suffix, *field* + *-ed* and *field* + *-er*. Further patterns consist of more than one suffix, as in *educational*, built out of *educate* + *-ion* + *-al*, or a prefix and a stem, as in *overlook*.

Phrases, as we saw in Chapter 2 on constituent structure, are given a special interpretation in linguistics and may consist of just one word; *she* and *John* are noun phrases. Many phrases consist of more than one word; for example *our new colleague's car*, *the car of our new colleague* and *a car of our new colleague's*. These three constructions are not equivalent in meaning; for instance, the last one is used only in situations in which the new colleague referred to has more than one car. A different choice of words brings out differences in meaning; *the book of the month* is the normal phrase while *the month's book* is unacceptable; *the idea of leaving (is ridiculous)* is acceptable while *Leaving's idea is ridiculous* is bizarre unless *Leaving* is somebody's name.

3.2 Different constructions and different meanings

We focus here on constructions in clauses. Two ideas are central to our discussion. The first is that we can recognise basic clauses and more complex clauses and can work out the relationships between them. That is, constructions are not isolated structures but fit into a general network.

The second idea is that different constructions exist, or have been created by the speakers and writers of given languages, to enable speakers and writers to signal what they are doing with a particular utterance. This connection between different constructions and different acts performed by speakers and writers is also central in the discussion of meaning and word classes/parts of speech in Chapter 4. We first examine a number of different constructions in English and then consider the question of the relationships among them.

Consider the examples in (1).

(1) a. The wealthy young man bought that piano for his secret fiancée.
   b. Did the wealthy young man buy that piano for his secret fiancée?

Example (1a) and (1b) are clearly related. They are related semantically in that they both have to do with a situation in which one person, a wealthy young man, bought something, a piano, for another person, his secret fiancée. Both examples place that situation at some point in past time, and both present the event as completed. The young man completed the purchase of the piano, whereas *was buying that piano* would have left it open whether the purchase was completed or not. The semantic relationship is indicated by three properties of the examples. They share the major lexical items, *wealthy, young, man, buy, piano, secret* and *fiancée*; in both examples, *wealthy* and *young* modify *man* and *secret* modifies *fiancée*; and *buy* has as its complements *the wealthy young man*, referring to the buyer, *that piano*, referring to the thing bought, and *his secret fiancée*, referring to the recipient of the piano. Note that although (1a) contains *bought* and (1b) contains *buy* these are both forms of one and same lexical item.

Both examples share past tense, which is marked on *bought* in (1a) and on *did* in (1b). The two examples differ in that (1b) has *did* at the beginning of the clause while (1a) does not. The presence or absence of *did* is immaterial for the semantics as discussed so far because it has no effect on the type of event – buying, on the participants involved in the event, on whether the event is presented as completed or on the time of the event. The presence or absence of *did* at the front of the clause signals a difference in the speaker's or writer's attitude to the event; (1a) is used in order to assert or declare that the event took place, while (1b) is used in order to ask if the event did take place. (We ignore the various nuances of meaning that can be signalled in spoken language by changes in intonation and stress and that might signalled in writing by the use of italics or bold or underlining.)

Example (1a) is an instance of a declarative construction (reflecting the idea that the speaker or writer declares something to be the case);

(1b) is an example of an interrogative construction, used by speakers who wish to ask whether the event took place, that is, speakers who wish to interrogate the person or persons they are addressing (their addressees). Other interrogative constructions are used when speakers know that a particular type of event took place but not the identity of one or more participants. Consider the examples in (2).

(2) a. Who bought that piano for his secret fiancée?
    b. What did the wealthy young man buy for his secret fiancée?
    c. Who did the wealthy young man buy that piano for?

Examples (2a–c) are not directly related in meaning to (1a–b), for the simple reason that (1a–b) specify all the participants in the buying event – the wealthy young man, the piano and the secret fiancée. In (2a–c), one of the participants is unknown. It makes more sense to consider (2a) as related in meaning to *Someone bought a piano for his secret fiancée* and (2b) as related in meaning to *The wealthy young man bought something for his secret fiancée*. (Note that *Someone bought that piano for his secret fiancée* has the same general syntactic structure as (1a), namely a noun phrase – *the wealthy young man* in (1a), then the verb and then a prepositional phrase *for his secret fiancée*.) The syntactic changes are slightly more complex. Where the identity of the buyer is requested, as in (2a), the noun phrase *someone* is replaced by *who*. Where the identity of another participant is requested, *someone* is replaced by *who* and *something* is replaced by *what*. *Who* and *what* move to the front of the clause, and *did* is inserted into the clause just following *who* or *what*.

Returning to (1a), we see that other constructions are related to it (more accurately, to the construction exemplified in it). Consider (3).

(3) The wealthy young man bought his secret fiancée that piano.

What has changed is that the preposition *for* is missing and *that piano* has swapped places with *his secret fiancée*. Example (3) might be used when the fiancée has already been mentioned and the piano is being introduced into the conversation; (1a) is more likely to be used when the piano has already been mentioned and it is the fiancée who is being brought into the narrative. The semantic difference between these two constructions is minimal; the distinction has to do with which participant has already been mentioned and with which is being mentioned for the first time. The syntactic structure of (3) is the subject noun phrase *the wealthy young man*, followed by the verb *bought*, followed by the noun phrase *his secret fiancée* and finally the noun phrase *that piano*.

We can usefully note that (3) adds another factor to our view of language. We stated at the beginning of this chapter that different constructions have been developed by the speakers of languages to allow them to distinguish clearly between the different things they do with language – making assertions, asking questions and so on. Example (3) drives home a very important point; although it is convenient in textbooks such as this to take **sentences** and clauses one at a time, in real speech and writing they are accompanied by many other clauses and sentences. The choice of the construction in (3) is determined by what precedes it in a given conversation or letter, say. In fact, to make the example more realistic, we should change it to *He bought her that piano*; one of the enduring habits of speakers is that they introduce a participant into a narrative by means of a full noun phrase containing a noun and possibly an article and adjective and so on, but thereafter refer to that participant by means of a **pronoun**. We might have a text as in (4).

(4) You were asking about the piano you saw. Frank Churchill was a wealthy young man who came to stay in Hartfield. His secret fiancée was living in Hartfield with Mrs and Miss Bates. He bought her that piano.

The fact that sentences are typically combined to create longer texts is why many manuals of languages include a selection of different texts in addition to the details of the morphology and syntax of a given language.

Utterance (1a) is an example of a **declarative clause**. It is also an example of an **active clause**, which contrasts with the corresponding passive clause in (5).

(5) That piano was bought for his secret fiancée by the wealthy young man.

Why call this a '**passive' clause**? The term 'passive' comes historically from the Latin verb *patior* (I suffer), or more exactly from its past participle, as in *passus sum* (having-suffered I-am, that is, 'I have suffered'). This label was chosen for clauses in English and other languages which take as their starting point the participant on whom an action is carried out, that is, who suffers the action. In contrast, active clauses take as their starting point the participant who carries out an action, who is active in a given situation.

Notice two properties of passive clauses. First, the noun phrase referring to the passive participant, *that piano* in (5), is at the front of the clause and is in a special relationship with the verb (agreement in person and number, discussed in Chapters 8 and 10). Second, although (5) does have a noun phrase, *the wealthy young man*, referring to the buyer, it can be omitted, as in *That piano was bought for his secret fiancée*. The construction in (5) is called the '**long passive**' because it contains an agent noun phrase; but approximately 95 per cent of passive clauses in spoken and written texts do not have a phrase referring to the do-er or agent. Without its agent phrase, as in the above example *That piano was bought for his secret fiancée*, this construction is known as the '**short passive**'.

The final construction we look at is that of (6).

(6) (I don't like the plum brandy) – the port I just love

The clause in brackets provides a plausible context for the second clause. The speaker contrasts the two types of alcoholic drink, producing a normal neutral clause to pass judgement on the plum brandy and driving home the contrast by putting the direct object *the port* at the front of the second clause. Not only does the second clause have an unusual construction, which in itself makes the message conspicuous, but *the port* immediately follows *the plum brandy*; the positioning of the two phrases right next to each other also highlights the contrast. As far as the syntactic structure is concerned, *I just love the port* is a neutral main clause and the only change to the structure is that the phrase *the port* moves to the beginning of the clause.

In the discussion of (3) above, we observed that, although we analyse clauses and sentences individually for convenience, in real language they do not occur in isolation but as part of longer texts. Constructions too can be and are analysed in isolation because it is convenient to focus on one structure at a time; however, in a given language, constructions exist not in isolation but as part of a system of structures. We finish this chapter by addressing the question 'What is meant by "system"?' and we do so on the basis of the six structures discussed above. To facilitate the discussion, the six structures are exemplified in (7) and (8) by means of simpler sentences.

3.3 Types of construction

The different constructions are labelled, and the labelling reflects the connections among them. The constructions can be represented in the form of a hierarchy, as in Figure 3.1 in Appendix 3. A major split is between constructions, such as (11a–c) below, that have the verb BE (traditionally called the **copula** or link verb) and constructions that have an 'ordinary' verb. Both copula and non-copula constructions can be **declarative**, that is, they can have the structure used for making statements, and **interrogative**, that is, they can have the structure used for asking questions.

Interrogative constructions split into two types. **YES–NO interrogatives** are used for asking questions such as *Did he phone?*, to which the answer is *yes* or *no*. **WH interrogatives** are used for asking questions about participants in a situation: *Who phoned?*, *When did he phone?*, *What did he say?*, *Where was he when he phoned?*

Declarative constructions can be both active, as in (7a), and passive, as in (7c). Interrogative constructions can be active, as in (8a), or passive, as in (8c). In declarative constructions, the verb can be followed by a noun phrase and a prepositional phrase, as in *bought the piano for Jane* in (7a), or by two noun phrases, as in *bought Jane the piano* in (7b). The former construction is here labelled OBLIQUE OBJECT and the latter is labelled DOUBLE OBJECT. Interrogative constructions can be OBLIQUE OBJECT, as in *Did Frank buy the piano for Jane?* in (8a), or DOUBLE OBJECT, as in *Did Frank buy Jane the piano?* in (8b). In turn, the DOUBLE OBJECT construction can be active or passive – *Frank bought Jane the piano* in (7b) and *Jane was bought that piano by Frank*; the OBLIQUE OBJECT construction too can be active or passive – *Frank bought the piano for Jane* (7a) and *The piano was bought for Jane by Frank* (7c).

(7) a. Frank bought the piano for Jane.
    [NON-COPULA, DECLARATIVE, ACTIVE, OBLIQUE OBJECT]

   b. Frank bought Jane the piano.
    [NON-COPULA, DECLARATIVE, ACTIVE, DOUBLE OBJECT]

   c. The piano was bought for Jane by Frank.
    [NON-COPULA, DECLARATIVE, PASSIVE, OBLIQUE OBJECT]

   d. The piano Frank bought for Jane.
    [NON-COPULA, DECLARATIVE, ACTIVE, OBLIQUE OBJECT, TOPIC]

(8) a. Did Frank buy the piano for Jane?
    [NON-COPULA, INTERROGATIVE, YES–NO, ACTIVE, OBLIQUE OBJECT]

   b. Did Frank buy Jane the piano?
    [NON-COPULA, INTERROGATIVE, YES–NO, ACTIVE, DOUBLE OBJECT]

   c. Was the piano bought for Jane by Frank?
    [NON-COPULA, INTERROGATIVE, PASSIVE, OBLIQUE OBJECT, YES–NO]

3.4 Relationships between constructions

Two central ideas lie behind the use of the word 'system'. One is that each of the above constructions shares certain properties with some of the other constructions; the other is that it is possible to specify the relationships between the constructions. The above constructions fall into two major classes, the DECLARATIVE constructions in (7) and the INTERROGATIVE constructions in (8). It is generally accepted that the DECLARATIVE ACTIVE construction in (7a) is basic. It is the most frequent type of construction in English, because speakers most often make assertions, indeed assertions about agents, and it allows the widest range of modifications – for example, *Frank had been buying the piano for Jane* is perfectly acceptable, and even *The piano had been being bought by Frank,* though awkward, can be used in texts instead of the unmodified passive, although the texts do not run as smoothly. Examples of the basic construction allow the widest range of adverbs and are semantically basic; the interpretations of *Did Frank deceive Emma?* and *Frank didn't deceive Emma* both involve an understanding of *Frank deceived Emma,* to which is added an understanding of what is signalled by the interrogative syntax and of what is signalled by the negative *didn't.*

The basic construction in (7a) is related to the other constructions in (7b–c) and also to the interrogative constructions in (8). We can think of the relationships among the constructions as paths that lead from the basic construction to the others. Do we lay out paths from the basic construction to every other one, say from the construction in (7a) to the constructions in (7b), (8a) and (8c)? The answer is 'no'. Instead, we lay out paths from the basic DECLARATIVE construction to the other DECLARATIVE constructions, and then we will put down paths from each of the DECLARATIVE constructions to the corresponding INTERROGATIVE one. Thus a path goes from (7a) to the [DOUBLE OBJECT] construction in (7b) and another path goes from (7b) to the [DOUBLE OBJECT] INTERROGATIVE construction in (8b). Another path goes from the construction in (7a) to the [NON-COPULA, DECLARATIVE, PASSIVE, OBLIQUE OBJECT] construction in (7c). From (7c), a path goes to the [NON-COPULA, INTERROGATIVE, YES–NO, PASSIVE, OBLIQUE OBJECT] construction in (8c). A path goes from (7a) to the construction in (7d), but there is no corresponding [NON-COPULA, INTERROGATIVE, TOPIC] construction for a path to lead to.

What about the constructions in (2)? As explained above, these are WH interrogatives, and a simpler version of (2b) is given in (9).

(9) What did Frank buy for Jane?
     [NON-COPULA,   INTERROGATIVE,   WH,   ACTIVE,
     OBLIQUE OBJECT]

In the discussion of (2a–c), we saw that (9) relates not to *Frank bought a piano for Jane* but to *Frank bought something for Jane*. The speaker knows that Frank bought and Jane received a present and asks for the present to be specified. We have three constructions to connect, shown in (10).

(10) a. Frank bought something for Jane.
          [NON-COPULA, DECLARATIVE, ACTIVE, OBLIQUE
          OBJECT]

      b. Did Frank buy something for Jane.
          [NON-COPULA, INTERROGATIVE, YES–NO, ACTIVE,
          OBLIQUE OBJECT]

      c. What did Frank buy for Jane.
          [NON-COPULA,   INTERROGATIVE,   WH,   ACTIVE,
          OBLIQUE OBJECT]

As before, we avoid paths going independently from the construction in (10a) to the constructions in (10b) and (10c). Instead, we will lay down a path from (10a) to (10b) and a path from (10b) to (10c). This captures the fact that (10b) and (10c) have something in common, the occurrence of the auxiliary verb *did* before the subject *Frank*. It also captures the fact that in syntactic terms (10c) is further away from (10a) than (10b), since not only is there the auxiliary verb *did* preceding the subject *Frank*, but (10c) also contains the WH pronoun *what*.

3.5 Copula constructions

We close this chapter with a quick look at copula constructions. Note that the division between COPULA and NON-COPULA constructions is the topmost one; constructions are divided into COPULA and NON-COPULA, then each of these divides into DECLARATIVE and INTERROGATIVE, and so on. Whether passives are COPULA or NON-COPULA is a moot point. Example (8c) certainly contains *was*, but the analysis turns on whether *was* is treated as a separate copula word or whether *was given* is treated as simply the passive form of *give*. We will treat passives as NON-COPULA because a number of constituents can occur in passives that are typically excluded from copula clauses, for example adverbs such as *immediately*.

(11) COPULA CONSTRUCTIONS
    a. NP Copula AP   Fiona is very happy.
                                        [COPULA, ASCRIPTIVE]
    b. NP Copula NP   Fiona is the best student.
                                        [COPULA, EQUATIVE]
    c. NP Copula PP   Fiona is in Auchtermuchty.
                                        [COPULA, LOCATIVE]

'Copula' is the Latin word for 'link, connection'. The motivation for the different label is that the constructions in (11), and their Latin equivalents, do not describe situations in which one participant performs an action, possibly on another person or thing. Rather, the verb *is* merely links the subject noun phrase with another phrase, in this case an adjective phrase *very happy* in (11a), a noun phrase *the best student* in (11b) and a prepositional phrase *in Auchtermuchty* in (11c).

Ascriptive copula clauses are used to ascribe a property to an entity. In (11a), happiness is ascribed to Fiona. Equative copula clauses are used to state that one entity is identical with another entity. Speakers use (11b) to say, on the assumption that there are two entities Fiona and the best student, that these two entities are one and the same person. Fiona is equated to the best student. The label [COPULA, LOCATIVE] is self-explanatory; this construction is used in order to state where some entity is located.

The copula constructions display a number of peculiarities compared with the (in)transitive constructions. Examples (11a–c) cannot be made passive; and, at least according to the handbooks of standard written English, the pronoun that is the complement of the copula is in the 'nominative' form: *It was I/he/she.* (But *It was we* and *It was they* sound peculiar.) *Is* can be moved to the front of the clause to make an interrogative – *Is Fiona the best student?* In this respect, *is* resembles *has* as used in some varieties: *Has Fiona a car?* But *have* combines with *do* for emphasis – *Fiona does have a car* – and also in interrogatives – *Does Fiona have a car? Be* does not combine with *do* (at least, not in standard English, whether written or spoken): **Fiona does be the best student, *Does Fiona be the best student?*

Implicit in the preceding paragraph is the fact that copula clauses can be declarative or interrogative, and they can be YES–NO or WH interrogatives – *Is she coming to the party?* vs *Who is coming to the party?* Unlike non-copula clauses, copula clauses cannot be passive and they do not have double objects, though they can have oblique objects as in *This parcel is for Sarah.* The complements of *be* are not usually treated as direct objects but are simply called complements. And as (11a) and (11c) show, *be* is regularly complemented by adjectives or by prepositional phrases.

Summary

Phrases combine to produce clauses. They combine in different orders, and the links between them are marked in various ways that will be discussed in Chapter 9. Some clauses have special markers such as *do, does, did* for YES–NO INTERROGATIVES or conjunctions such as *although, if* and *that*, to be discussed in Chapter 6. The above differences are said to reflect different constructions; phrases are constructed or put together in different ways to enable speakers and writers to signal differences in meaning. The various syntactic constructions in a given language form a system; one task of syntactic analysis is to work out and state how the constructions are interconnected.

Exercises

1. The discussion in this chapter identified a number of constructions: COPULA and NON-COPULA, DECLARATIVE and INTERROGATIVE, YES–NO and WH INTERROGATIVES, ACTIVE and PASSIVE, DOUBLE OBJECT and OBLIQUE OBJECT and, for declaratives only, TOPIC and NON-TOPIC. COPULA clauses are ASCRIPTIVE, EQUATIVE or LOCATIVE. For each of the following sentences, decide its construction and label it using the labels given above. Thus, *Was Admiral Croft given a present by Lady Russell?* is classified as [NON-COPULA (it contains a copula but also an ordinary verb, *given*), INTERROGATIVE, YES–NO, PASSIVE, and OBLIQUE OBJECT]. Remember that non-basic constructions must be related to basic constructions. This is especially relevant to (10).

   1. Colonel Brandon read poems to Marianne.
   2. Mrs Gardiner was Mrs Bennet's sister.
   3. Who was Jane Bennet's suitor?
   4. Why did Frank Churchill deceive everybody?
   5. When was Emma scolded by Mr Knightley?
   6. Was Mr Knightley much older than Emma?
   7. Where did Captain Wentworth propose to Anne Elliott?
   8. Sir Walter Elliott was in Bath.
   9. Did Colonel Brandon bring Marianne books?
   10. Elizabeth Bennet was at first unimpressed with Mr D'Arcy.

2. Devise examples of constructions that fit the following labels. For instance, an example of (1) is *Jane is in Toorak*.

1. [COPULA, DECLARATIVE, LOCATIVE]
2. [NON-COPULA, DECLARATIVE, PASSIVE]
3. [NON-COPULA, INTERROGATIVE, YES–NO, DOUBLE OBJECT]
4. [COPULA, INTERROGATIVE, YES–NO, ASCRIPTIVE]
5. [NON-COPULA, INTERROGATIVE, WH, PASSIVE]
6. [COPULA, INTERROGATIVE, WH, EQUATIVE]

4 Word classes

4.1 What are word classes?

In the preceding chapters, we have used terms such as 'noun', 'adjective', 'adverb', 'verb' and 'preposition' without defining them. The terms are in everyday use and everyday definitions are available, such as nouns being the names of persons, places and things and verbs being the names of actions or states. These definitions contain a grain of truth but are inadequate for serious investigation of English or any other language. One weakness is that they appeal in a superficial way to only one part of meaning, the kind of things that a given word denotes. As we will see in Section 4.2.4, 'Semantic criteria', it is important to take account of what speakers and writers actually do with verbs, nouns and so on. (The term 'denote' is used for the relationship between a given word and the set of entities, in the broadest sense, to which it can be applied. Traditional dictionary explanations of the meaning of individual words can be thought of as embryo descriptions of denotations. In the last section of this chapter (4.2.5), we see that, for example, nouns are the centre of noun phrases, by means of which speakers and writers refer to entities.)

Another weakness is that they ignore the business of where a given word is placed in a clause or phrase, a topic which was introduced in the discussion of phrases in Chapter 2 but which is also important for the analysis of words. For a given word, we can investigate what words it typically combines with in phrases, what types of phrase it occurs in and where these types of phrase occur in clauses. For instance, nouns can be preceded by words such as *the*, *a* and *this* but verbs cannot. Adjectives can precede a noun, as in *new books*, or follow certain verbs, as in *is new*, *seemed new*. Verbs occur in different slots in the clause. That is, we transfer from humans to words the precept that you know them by the company they keep and group them into classes, hence the term 'word classes'.

We appeal first to a very old distinction between words that have a denotation and words that do not. Words that have a denotation apply to people, places, things (in the broadest sense), actions, states and properties. They are known as **lexical** or **content words**, and in English include nouns (e.g. *villa, baby, idea*), verbs (e.g. *buy, destroy, think*), adjectives (e.g. *wooden, strong, abstract*) and adverbs (e.g. *rapidly, hopefully*). Words that do not refer are known as **grammatical** or **form words**. ('Lexical' usually contrasts with 'grammatical', 'content' with 'form'.) Grammatical or form words in English are the definite and indefinite articles *the* and *a*, the demonstrative adjectives *this, these, that* and *those*, the **auxiliary verbs** *is, has* and so on (as in *is reading a book, has read this book*). (The term 'auxiliary' reflects the fact that these verbs do not refer to actions or states but 'help' main verbs such as *read* to build a construction.)

Many accounts of word classes in English treat verbs such as *may, could* and *must* and prepositions such as *with, from* and *by* as grammatical words, but these seem to be on the borderline. In the days before widespread telephone communication and before the invention of fax machines and e-mail, urgent messages were sent by telegram. Each word cost a certain amount, and to keep down the cost of the whole telegram people put in only those words essential for the message to be interpreted correctly. For instance, instead of *We are arriving on Tuesday at 5pm* the telegram would read *Arriving Tuesday 5pm*. The words that typically turned up in telegrams were nouns, verbs and (less often) adjectives and adverbs, namely content words. Articles, demonstrative adjectives, auxiliary verbs and prepositions were typically left out.

The problem is that, in spite of the telegram test, the distinction between *Press the button above the green light* and *Press the button below the green light* is rather important; the prepositions *above* and *below* cannot be left out, because a wrong interpretation might lead to just as regrettable consequences as the difference between *Press the red button* and *Press the green button*. What the telegram test shows is that some missing words can be easily guessed while others cannot. Prepositions such as *on* and *at* in time phrases have no competitors – the sender of the telegram might have meant *after 5pm*, but we would expect *after* or *before* to be stated explicitly in the message. Prepositions such as *below* have competitors such as *above, next, by, opposite*; recent analyses of prepositions have shown that many have major meanings and can only be described as words with denotations. Equally, we must concede that the meaning of a preposition such as *of* is hard to establish. For these reasons, and in spite of the telegram test, prepositions (along with modal verbs such as *can* and *must*) will be regarded as lexical or content words. In this class of lexical items, they are not as central as nouns, say, but they are not grammatical items either such as *the* and *a*.

4.2 Criteria for word classes

Four types of criteria are employed to set up word classes – syntactic, **morphological**, **morpho-syntactic** and semantic. (Semantic criteria have to do with meaning.) We begin with a brief explanation of morphological and morpho-syntactic criteria, which have to do with what is called **inflectional morphology**. Consider the English examples *The tiger is smiling* and *The tigers are smiling*. The contrast between *tiger* and *tigers* shows that *tigers* can be split into *tiger* and *-s*. *Tiger* is the stem and *-s* is the suffix added to the end of the stem. The stem *tiger* is a noun and the addition of *-s* does not affect this property. In contrast, the addition of *-ish* does affect it; *tiger* is a noun but *tigerish* is an adjective. In dictionaries of English, *tigerish* and *tigers* are treated differently. *Tigerish* is listed as a separate lexical item, that is, it might be listed in the same entry as *tiger* but appear in bold and with a short explanation of its meaning; *tigers* has no entry at all, since the makers of dictionaries assume that users will know how to convert the singular form of a given noun to a plural form.

Suffixes such as *-ish* that derive new lexical items are **derivational suffixes**; suffixes that express grammatical information, such as 'plural', are inflectional suffixes. (The term comes from the Latin verb *flectere* 'to bend' and is connected with the idea that, in languages such as Russian with a multitude of inflectional suffixes, nouns, verbs and adjectives have a basic form that is bent by the addition of a suffix.) There is one more property of inflectional suffixes: in the *tiger* clauses above, *tiger* combines with *is smiling* and *tigers* combines with *are smiling*. That is, there is linkage between subject noun and verb. Traditionally, a distinction is drawn between agreement and government; these topics will be discussed in Chapter 9.

4.2.1 Morphological criterion

The singular form *criterion* is used in the heading because what is at stake is simply whether a given word allows grammatical suffixes or not. This criterion is the least important of the four listed above and is more relevant to some languages than others. It is of the greatest interest with respect to languages such as Russian, in which nouns have different suffixes ('endings' in the traditional, informal terminology) depending on their relationship to the verb. Examples are given in (1).

(1) a. Sobaka lajala
        dog   barked   'The dog barked.'

b. Koshka tsarapala sobaku
   cat   scratched dog   'The cat scratched the dog.'

c. Petr dal   sobake kost'
   Peter gave dog   bone   'Peter gave the dog a bone.'

The noun *sobaka* in (1a) splits into the stem *sobak-* and the suffix *-a*, which here signals the animal doing the barking. In (1b), *sobak-* has its direct object suffix *-u*, which here marks the animal being scratched; in (1c), it has its oblique object suffix *-e*, which here marks the recipient of the bone. A few nouns in Russian take no suffixes, for example *taksi* (taxi), *kofe* (coffee) and *kakadu* (cockatoo). (Such nouns do not vary their shape and are called invariable words.) English does not have the same range of grammatical suffixes as Russian, but English nouns typically take a plural ending – *fish–fishes*, *cat–cats* and *dog–dogs*. (The *-s* represents different suffixes in speech – in *cats* it represents the initial sound of *speed*, in *dogs* the initial sound of *zap*.) Some nouns in English do not take a plural suffix – for example *sheep*, *deer* – and are said to be invariable.

4.2.2 Morpho-syntactic criteria

These criteria have to do with inflectional suffixes, as described above in connection with the *tiger* examples, and the information signalled by them, and were developed on the basis of languages such as Classical Latin and Classical Greek. We looked at Russian examples above because Russian is not only very like Latin and Greek in its richness of inflectional suffixes but is also a living language. It will be helpful to take a further look at Russian before returning to English.

Examples (1a–c) show that nouns in Russian take different suffixes which signal the relationship between the nouns and the verb in a clause. (See Chapters 10 and 11 for a discussion of these relationships.) These relationships are known as case, and nouns are said to be inflected for the category of case. ('Case' derives from the Latin word for a fall, *casus*. The basic form of a noun, such as *sobaka* in (1a) – the subject form; see Chapter 8 – was thought of as upright, and the other forms were thought of as falling away from the subject form.) Other information is signalled by case suffixes in Indo-European languages. Consider (2).

(2) a. Sobaki lajut
       dogs   bark   'The dogs are barking.'

    b. Petr dal   kost' sobakam
       Peter gave bone to-dogs   'Peter gave a bone to the dogs.'

In (2a), *sobaki* is the subject but also plural, and it has a different suffix, *-i*. In (2b), *sobakam* refers to the recipient and is plural and it too has a different suffix from the one in (1c), *-am*. That is, the case suffixes actually signal information about case and about number.

Verbs in Russian signal information about time, person and number, as illustrated in (3).

(3) a. govorit o   Moskve
       speaks   about Moscow   'He/she is speaking about Moscow.'

    b. govorjat o   Moskve
       speak   about Moscow   'They are speaking about Moscow.'

    c. govorju o   Moskve
       speak-I about Moscow   'I am speaking about Moscow.'

    d. govorili o   Moskve
       spoke   about Moscow   'They were speaking about Moscow.'

Examples (3a–d) all refer to an event of speaking about Moscow: (3a) and (3b) place that event in present time; the speaker, as it were, says 'I am speaking to you now and they are speaking about Moscow'. Example (3d) presents the event in past time; the speaker can be imagined as saying 'I am speaking to you now and at some before this they were speaking about Moscow'. Information about the time of an event is signalled by the difference in form between *govorit* and *govorjat* on the one hand and *govorili* on the other, the *l* in *govorili* indicating past time. Such differences in verbs are said to express tense.

Example (3a) contains *govorit*, and (3b) contains *govorjat*. Both are said to be in the third person; in the traditional scheme, first person is the speaker, at the centre of any piece of interaction by means of language; close to the centre is second person, the person(s) addressed by the speaker. Other participants, or other people or things talked about by the speaker, are third persons. The contrasts in form are said to express person. (The term 'person' is not entirely appropriate for animals or inanimate objects, but human beings tend to place human beings at the centre of their thinking about the world; typical conversation is taken to be by human beings about human beings.)

Returning to (3a) and (3b), (3a) presents the speaking as being done by one person, (3b) presents it as being done by more than one person. These contrasts are said to express number (as does a different set of contrasts in the shape of nouns, as illustrated in (1) and (2).

In the languages regarded as native to Europe (belonging mostly to the Indo-European and Finno-Ugric families), the words classed as nouns carry information about number and, in some languages, about case; words classed as verbs carry information about tense, person and number (and some other types of information not mentioned here – for a more detailed discussion, see Chapter 13). In traditional terms, nouns are inflected for case and number, and verbs are inflected for tense, person and number. In some languages, adjectives too are inflected for case and number. Adverbs and prepositions are typically not inflected, though some prepositions in the Celtic languages (Scottish and Irish Gaelic, Welsh and Breton (also Cornish in Cornwall and Manx in the Isle of Man) do have inflected forms as a result of historical change. It is as though in English the sequences *to me* and *to you* had coalesced into what were perceived as single words, *tme* and *tyou* (the latter probably pronounced *chew*).

English does not have the rich system of inflections possessed by languages such as Russian, but English nouns do take suffixes expressing number (*cat* and *cats*, *child* and *children* and so on), and English verbs do take suffixes expressing tense: *pull* and *pulls* vs *pulled*. There are of course nouns, such as *mouse–mice*, that express number by other means, and there are verbs, such as *write–wrote*, *eat–ate*, that express tense by other means. Person is expressed only by the *-s* suffix added to verbs in the present tense – *pulls*, *writes* and so on. Of course, English verbs cannot occur on their own in declarative clauses but require at least one noun phrase, which could consist of just a personal pronoun – *I, you, he, she, it, we, they*. To the extent that English verbs require a noun phrase, which is often a personal pronoun (in 65 per cent of clauses in spontaneous spoken English), we are entitled to regard person as a category intrinsic to the verb in English. (Non-personal pronouns, that is nouns, are by definition third person.)

English adjectives are not associated with number or case, but many of them take suffixes signalling a greater quantity of some property (for example *bigger*) or the greatest quantity of some property (for example *biggest*). These morpho-syntactic properties of English words, signalling information about tense, person and number, are presented in this chapter as relevant to the recognition of different word classes, but as we will see in Chapter 8 they are also relevant to linkage (agreement and government), as mentioned at the beginning of this chapter.

4.2.3 Syntactic criteria

The syntactic criteria for word classes are based on what words a given word occurs with and the types of phrase in which a given word occurs. Syntactic criteria are the most important. They are important for

English with its relative poverty of morpho-syntactic criteria, and they are crucial for the analysis of word classes in general because there are languages such as Mandarin Chinese which have practically no inflectional suffixes (such as plural endings); in contrast, all languages have syntax.

The recognition of syntactic criteria as central is a major step forward, but the application of these criteria is not straightforward. Consider the English words that are called nouns. They all have several properties in common, namely they can occur in various positions relative to the verb in a clause. Examples (4a–c) are instances of the [NON-COPULA, ACTIVE, DECLARATIVE] construction described in Chapter 3.

(4) a.   The dog stole the turkey.
    b.   The children chased the dog.
    c.   The cook saved no scraps for the dog.

Dog occurs to the left of *stole* in (4a), to the right of *chased* in (4b), and to the right of *saved* in (4c) but separated from it by the intervening word *for*. *Dog* also occurs in a noun phrase and can be modified by a word such as *the* – *The dog stole the turkey* – or by an adjective – *Hungry dogs stole the turkey* – or by *the* and an adjective together – *The hungry dogs stole the turkey*.

All other nouns in English can occur to the left of the verb in an active declarative clause, but not all nouns combine with an article, or combine with articles in the same way as *dog* does. (This property of nouns has already been mentioned in Chapter 1 in connection with dependency relations and the idea that different nouns require or allow different types of word inside a noun phrase.) *Dog stole the turkey* is unacceptable (assuming *Dog* is not a proper name), whereas *Ethel stole the turkey* is not. The difficulty is that the class of English nouns is a very large class of words that do not all keep the same company (or, to use another metaphor, do not all behave in the same way). All nouns meet the criteria of occurring to the left of a verb in an active declarative clause, of occurring immediately to the right of a verb in an active declarative clause or of occurring to the right of a verb but preceded by a preposition. These are major criteria, but there are the minor criteria mentioned above, such as combining with an article, or being able to occur without an article, or not allowing a plural suffix (*Ethels*). These split the class of nouns into subclasses.

A sufficiently detailed examination of the company kept by individual nouns would probably reveal that each noun has its own pattern of occurrence. Thanks to very large electronic bodies of data and the search power of computers, analysts are beginning to carry out such examinations and to find such individual patterns. For the purposes of

analysing syntax, however, it is not helpful to gather information about individual nouns and it is impossible to produce a useable analysis of English syntax (or the syntax of any other language) with, say, 20,000 word classes. To analyse and discuss the general syntactic structure of clauses and sentences, we need fairly general classes, and analysts try to keep to major criteria plus those minor criteria that lead to relatively large classes of words. For other purposes, such as compiling a dictionary, smaller classes are required, down to information about individual words. (See Chapter 5 on the lexicon.)

A concept that is central to discussion of word classes, and indeed to any class of items, linguistic or non-linguistic, is that of the **central and peripheral members of a class**. Consider the adjective *tall* in the examples in (5).

(5) a.   a tall building
    b.   This building is tall.
    c.   a very tall building
    d1. a taller building
    d2. a more beautiful building

There are two criteria labelled 'd' because some adjectives take the comparative suffix *-er* while others do not allow that suffix but require *more*. Some adjectives, like *tall*, meet all the criteria in (5) and are central or prototypical members of the class. Some adjectives fail to meet all the criteria. *Unique* satisfies (5a–c), as in *a unique building, This building is unique* and *a very unique building*. (Publishers' copy-editors might object to *very unique*, but the combination occurs regularly in speech and in informal writing and even in newspapers.) *Unique* does not combine with *-er* or *more*: *a uniquer building, *a more unique building*. In the class of adjectives, *unique* is slightly less central than *tall*. *Woollen* meets even fewer criteria. *A woollen cloak* and *This cloak is woollen* are acceptable, but *a woollener cloak, *a more woollen cloak* and *a very woollen cloak* are not. Woollen is less central than *unique*, which in turn is less central than *tall*. Right at the edge of the class is *asleep*, which meets only one of the criteria in (5), namely (5b). *The child is asleep* is acceptable but not *the asleep child, *the very asleep child, *the more asleep child*. On the other hand, *asleep* meets none of the criteria for nouns, verbs, prepositions or adverbs; it is a peripheral adjective.

4.2.4 Semantic criteria: what words mean

There are no semantic criteria, aspects of the meaning of the different classes of words, that would enable us to decide whether any given word is a noun, adjective, verb, adverb or preposition. We must accept right here that meaning cannot be exploited in this way. The traditional definition of nouns as words denoting people, places or things does not explain why words such as *anger, idea* or *death* are classified as nouns. *Race* the noun and *race* the verb both denote an event, as do the verb *transmit* in *They transmitted the concert live* and the noun *transmission* in *The live transmission of the concert.*

On the other hand, this book is based on the view that grammar is interesting because it plays an essential role in the communication of coherent messages of all sorts. It has been demonstrated many times that humans cannot (easily) remember meaningless symbols such as random sequences of words or numbers, like telephone numbers and PIN numbers. Psycholinguists know that children cannot learn sequences of symbols without meaning. It would be surprising were there no parallels at all between patterns of grammar and semantic patterns; we abandon the traditional notion that classes of words can be established on the basis of what words denote, but careful analysis does bring out patterns. The analysis uses the ideal of central, prototypical members of word classes as opposed to peripheral members, and it focuses on what speakers and writers do with words rather than on the traditional dictionary meanings.

The key move in the investigation of word classes is to accept that word classes must be defined on the basis of formal criteria – their morphological properties, their morpho-syntactic properties and their syntactic properties. Only when these formal patterns have been established can we move on to investigate the connection between meaning and word classes.

How do formal criteria and the concept of central members of a word class help the investigation of meaning? Interestingly, the traditional description of nouns as referring to persons, places and things turns out to be adequate for central nouns. Nouns such as *girl, town* and *car* combine with *the* and *a*, take the plural suffix -*s*, are modified by adjectives and occur to the left or the right of the verb in [NON-COPULA, ACTIVE DECLARATIVE] clauses. They also refer to observable entities such as people, places and things. What is significant is the combination of syntactic and morpho-syntactic properties with the semantic property of referring to people, places or things.

Many analysts argue that nouns such as *anger, property* and *event* do not denote things. However, these nouns do possess all or many of the syntactic and morpho-syntactic properties possessed by *girl, town* and *car*: *a property, the properties, an interesting property, invent properties, This property surprised us* and so on. *Anger* meets some of the major criteria –

The anger frightened him [subject, and combination with *the*] but not **an anger*. The fact that the major formal criteria for prototypical nouns apply to words such as *property* and *anger* is what justifies the latter being classed as nouns. On the assumption that these formal properties are not accidental, it also suggests that 'ordinary speakers' of English treat *anger* as though it denoted an entity.

A discussion of the linguistic and cognitive issues would be inappropriate here. What cannot be emphasised enough is that a word's classification as noun, verb and so on is on the basis of formal criteria; the terms 'noun', 'verb' and so on are merely labels for classes which could be replaced by neutral labels such as 'Class 1', 'Class 2' and so on. Words apparently very diverse in meaning such as *anger* and *dog* share many major syntactic and morpho-syntactic properties, and this raises deep and interesting questions about how 'ordinary speakers' conceive the world. It leads to the unexpected conclusion that the traditional semantic definitions of word classes, while quite unsatisfactory as definitions, nonetheless reflect an important fact about language and how ordinary speakers understand the world around them.

The need for both formal and semantic criteria becomes quite clear in comparisons of two or more languages. Descriptions of Russian, say, contain statements about the formal properties of nouns and verbs in Russian; descriptions of English contain statements about nouns and verbs in English. But formal criteria do not allow the English words labelled 'noun' to be equated to the Russian words labelled 'noun'; the formal criteria for the English word class are completely different from the formal criteria for the Russian word class. In spite of this, analysts and learners of Russian as a second language find no difficulty in talking of nouns in English and nouns in Russian and in equating the two. The basis for this behaviour must be partly semantic; central nouns in Russian (according to the Russian formal criteria) denote persons, places and things, and so do central nouns in English.

4.2.5 Semantic criteria: what speakers do with words

Even more important is what speakers and writers do with language. When they produce utterances, they perform actions. They act to produce sounds or marks on paper, but the purpose of producing the sounds (in many situations) is to draw the attention of their audience to some entity and to say something about it, to predicate a property of it. Examples of acts – let us use the generally accepted term **'speech acts'** – are making statements, asking questions and issuing commands (in the broadest sense). These speech acts are prominent in and central to human communication and are allotted grammatical resources in every language – see Chapter 3 on constructions. Other acts are not so prominent but are no less central to human communication and relate directly to the different parts of speech.

Two such speech acts are **referring** to entities and **predicating** properties of them. In English, the class of nouns, established on formal criteria, contains words denoting entities, and nouns enter into noun phrases, the units that speakers use when referring to entities. This is not to say that every occurrence of a noun phrase is used by a speaker to refer to something; nor is the difference between nouns and other word classes connected solely with referring; nonetheless, speakers require noun phrases in order to refer, and noun phrases can be used to refer only because they contain nouns.

The notion of **predication** as a speech act is prevalent in traditional grammar and is expressed in the formula of 'someone saying something about a person or thing'. Predication has been largely ignored in discussions of speech acts, perhaps because it is always part of a larger act, making a statement or asking a question or issuing a command. In English, verbs, including BE, signal the performance of a predication.

Whether adjectives and adverbs are associated with a speech act is a question that has not received much discussion. It is interesting, however, that in traditional grammar adjectives are also labelled 'modifiers', a label which reflects the function of these words in clauses. Speakers and writers use verbs to make an assertion about something, and the assertion involves assigning a property to that something. They use adjectives not to make an assertion but merely to add to whatever information is carried by the head noun in a given noun phrase.

Explaining the different word classes or parts of speech in terms of speech acts offers a solution to one difficulty with the traditional definitions; the class of things is so wide that it can be treated as including events; even properties, which are said to be referred to by adjectives, can be thought of as things. In contrast, different speech acts correspond to different word classes. The speech-act explanation also provides a connection between word classes in different languages. Assuming that basic communicative acts such as referring and predicating are recognised by speakers of different languages (communication between speakers of different languages would otherwise be impossible), the words classed as nouns in descriptions of, say, Russian, and the words classed as nouns in descriptions of, say, English, have in common that speakers pick words from those classes when referring. Similarly, speakers and writers pick what are called verbs when predicating, adjectives when adding to the information carried by a noun (that is, when they perform the speech act of modifying) and adverbs when they add to the information carried by a verb or an adjective.

We end this chapter with a comment on terminology. Linguists nowadays use the term 'word classes' and not the traditional term 'parts of speech'. 'Word classes' is neat and self-explanatory but is associated with the idea of words pinned down on the page or in the transcript of speech. 'Parts of speech' is not self-explanatory, but it does have the merit of reminding us that we are dealing not with dead text but with speakers and writers doing things with language.

Summary

The different classes of words – for example nouns, verbs, adjectives, adverbs, prepositions – were traditionally defined by what they denoted – people, places and things (nouns), actions (verbs) and properties (adjectives). This definition is inadequate, although meaning still has an important part to play. Reliable definitions are based on formal criteria – morphological (does a given word take inflectional suffixes or is it invariable?), morpho-syntactic (does a given word take suffixes having to do with person and number, or with case?) and syntactic (where in a phrase or clause does a given word occur?). Once formal criteria have been set up, the connection between word classes and meaning can be studied. This bears not just on what a given word or class of words refers to but also on what speakers and writers do with it – refer, predicate or assert, modify.

Exercises

1. Underline eight adjectives in the following passage.

   Decrepit Victorian mansions loomed out of the snowfall on the town's sporadic hills. Beyond them, cedars wove a steep mat of still green ... The wind drove snowflakes steadily inland, hurling them against the fragrant trees, and the snow began to settle on the highest branches with a gentle implacability.

Underline seven verbs in the following passage.

   By two o'clock on the first afternoon of the trial, snow covered all the island roads. A car pirouetted silently while skating on its tires, emerged from this on a transverse angle, and slid to a stop with one headlight thrust into the door of Petersen's Grocery, which somebody opened at just the right moment – miraculously – so that no damage befell car or store.

Both passages are from Dan Guterson, *Snow Falling on Cedars*.

2. We have seen that we can recognise a single class of verbs in English. In the neutral declarative construction, all verbs can occur to the right of a subject noun phrase (and, with a minute number of exceptions, verbs can be preceded by the infinitive marker *to* or be marked for tense, on the pattern of either *play–played* or *write–wrote*). Closer scrutiny reveals subclasses of verb. What constructions do the following verbs occur in? Think up examples using each verb and see how many different patterns you can devise. For example, if we were considering the verb HANG, we could devise examples such as *They hung the pictures on the wall opposite the window* or *They hung the wall with pictures* or *These curtains aren't hanging properly*.

    MEET   SCATTER   COLLIDE   CRASH

And the following verbs?

    MIX   BLEND   STIR

3. Classes of words consist of prototypical central members, peripheral members and some members that are neither one nor the other. For adjectives, we recognised four criteria exemplified in (5) above: occurring in a noun phrase (as an attributive adjective), occurring as the complement of a copula (as a predicative adjective), occurring with words such as *very* and occurring in the comparative, either with the suffix *-er* or with *more*. Of the adjectives listed below, which are central, prototypical adjectives, which are peripheral adjectives and which are in between?

    RICH   AWAKE   WOODEN   MAJOR

5 The lexicon

5.1 Syntax and lexical items

Why have a chapter on dictionaries in a book on syntax? The answer is simple and indisputable: syntax cannot be isolated from other areas of language; and individual lexical items, particularly verbs, exercise strong control over syntactic structure. We have already seen in Chapter 4 that when setting up word classes we have to appeal to syntactic criteria, to morphology and morpho-syntax and to meaning. In the very first chapter, we examined the idea that the head of a given phrase controls the other constituents in the phrase, and we saw immediately that there are different subclasses of nouns and verbs that impose different requirements on phrases and clauses. We saw only a small fraction of the extensive interplay between syntactic structure and individual lexical items; in this chapter again we can discuss only the main features, going into the topic in more detail but leaving huge areas untouched.

Analysts can isolate the syntactic constructions of a given language, as we started to do for English in Chapter 2 on constituent structure and in Chapter 3 on constructions. Syntactic constructions, however, are not identical with specific clauses; particular clauses do not appear until lexical items are inserted into a general syntactic structure. For example, the structure Noun Phrase–Verb–Noun Phrase corresponds to indefinitely many clauses: *The dog chewed its bone, The cat scratched the dog, Dogs like meat* and so on. The process of insertion is not simple. As mentioned above, particular lexical items only fit into particular pieces of structure – some verbs combine with one noun phrase, others with two, and a third set of verbs with three. Some singular nouns combine with *the* and *a*, and some exclude them. In addition there are many instances both of particular lexical items that typically combine with other specific lexical items (*rock hard*) and of **fixed phrases** (*know something like the back of one's hand*). Current searches of very large electronic bodies of text are beginning to reveal just how pervasive these restricted combinations and fixed phrases are.

Information about the interplay between lexical items and syntactic structure has always been available in all but the smallest dictionaries. *Chambers 20th Century Dictionary* (1983), for example, includes the following information in the entry for *knife*.

knife [*nīf*]; an instrument for cutting; *verb transitive*: to cut
  knifeless; *knifing* the act of putting a knife into someone
  war to the knife   *have one's knife in*

The entry gives some information about syntax; the verb is described as transitive, which means that in the basic ACTIVE DECLARATIVE construction it requires a noun phrase to its right. There is a rough guide to the pronunciation which does not use the International Phonetic Alphabet, a definition of the meaning of the noun, two words that are derived from the basic stem and two **idiomatic phrases**. The entry would not be very useful for a non-native speaker with a limited knowledge of English, but the dictionary is intended primarily for native speakers. The limitations become clear from the entry for *put*, which describes it as a transitive verb but does not say that *put* is different from *knife* in requiring a noun phrase and prepositional phrase to its right – *put the parcel on the table* vs *put the parcel*. The entry for *accuse* does not specify that it requires a noun phrase and a prepositional phrase to its right, nor that the preposition must be *of* – *Mandragora accused Panjandrum of plagiarism*.

This kind of information is supplied in dictionaries intended for schoolchildren and for people learning English as a second language, and must be included in adequate descriptions of English. What counts as an adequate description of a language? The major grammars of languages, particularly languages that are both spoken and written, include information about all the word, phrase, clause and sentence constructions in a large body of data, mostly drawn from written texts but nowadays likely to include transcripts of speech. The current most comprehensive grammar of English, *A Comprehensive Grammar of the English Language* by Sir Randolph Quirk et al. (1985), also includes information about how sentences combine to form larger texts and about typical or fixed combinations of lexical items.

Another approach to the writing of grammars has as its goal the writing of explicit rules, which 'generate' sentences. This task involves the writing of rules that specify syntactic constructions, it involves the writing of an accurate and detailed dictionary and it involves a detailed account of how the correct lexical item is inserted into a given syntactic structure and of how only acceptable combinations of lexical items are specified. This approach must also ensure that the rules do not specify unacceptable structures. This introduction does not aim at completely explicit rules, but we will exploit the idea of explicit rules and of a system of rules in order to organise our discussion of the lexicon. What is of crucial concern, of course, is the set of concepts to be used in the analysis of syntax (whether the syntax of English or of some other language); that is what this book focuses on.

5.2 Individual verbs, complements and adjuncts

In Chapter 1, we discussed the concepts of complement and adjunct. Every type of phrase has a head, and the modifiers of heads fall into the two classes of complement and adjunct. The distinction applies best to the modifiers of verbs, for which it was originally developed and which are the focus of Chapter 1. Complements are modifiers which typically occur next to the head (but not always) and which are required or excluded by particular lexical items. In (1), *Sarah* and *the cakes* are complements of *devoured*. *Devoured* requires a noun phrase to its left and a noun phrase to its right – *Sarah devoured* is unacceptable.

(1) Sarah devoured the cakes in the kitchen last night.

Adjuncts are not necessarily next to the head; indeed, they are typically at a distance from the verb. They are not obligatory. Whereas complements 'complete' the meaning of the verb, giving it both syntactic and semantic completion, adjuncts merely provide additional information that could be dispensed with. In (1) *in the kitchen* and *last night* are adjuncts; (1) is acceptable and complete without them – *Sarah devoured the cakes*. Adverbs of time and location are always adjuncts. Adverbs of location have to be distinguished from adverbs of direction (as per the discussion in Chapter 1); a verb such as *barge* requires a directional adverb – *Sarah barged into the kitchen* – and a verb such as *pushed* allows it – *Sarah pushed the pram* and *Sarah pushed the pram into the kitchen*. Even where a verb merely allows a **directional adverb**, the latter is a complement, because there are verbs that exclude them – *Sarah was cooking into the kitchen*. The fact that some (in fact, many) verbs exclude directional adverbs means that dictionary entries must include information about whether a given verb excludes an adverb of direction or not. This means that even for *push*, which allows rather than requires an adverb of direction, phrases such as *into the kitchen* are complements.

A given lexical verb controls various properties of its complements. Most obviously, it controls how many complements occur and what type of complements – noun phrases, adjective phrases, prepositional phrases or complement clauses. (We leave the term 'complement clause' unex-

plained just now; complement clauses are discussed in Chapter 6.)
Consider the examples in (2)–(5).

(2) a. Mr Knightley despaired.
    b. Emma slighted Miss Bates.
    c. Frank Churchill gave Jane Fairfax a piano.
(3)   Jane Fairfax seemed upset.
(4) a. Mr Woodhouse sat in an armchair.
    b. Mr Knightley walked into the drawing room.
    c. Mr Elton handed his wife into the carriage.
    d. Emma gave bad advice to Harriet.
(5)   Mr Knightley suggested that thieves would break into Hartfield
       House.

In (2a–c), *despaired* excludes a noun phrase to its right, *slighted* requires
one, and *gave* allows two noun phrases to its right. (We will see in
Chapter 8 that the first of these noun phrases, for example *Jane Fairfax*
in (2c), is felt to be less closely connected with the verb than the other
noun phrase.) In (3), *seemed* is a verb that requires some phrase, here
the adjective *upset*. A relatively small number of verbs allow adjective
complements. In (4a), *sat* (in the sense of 'was sitting' as opposed to 'sat
down') requires a prepositional phrase describing a location, here *in an
armchair*. Remember that the label 'prepositional phrase' relates to the
type of constituent, a phrase with a preposition as its head. In (4a), *in*
is the head of the prepositional phrase *in the armchair*, and *the armchair*
is the complement of *in*. Such phrases describing a location are said to
function as adverbs of location, which is a shorthand way of combining
information about their meaning and about their function – they modify
verbs. *Walked* in (4b) allows just a prepositional phrase describing a
direction, *into the drawing room*. (Note that this account of *sit* does not
contradict the statement that adverbs of location are typically adjuncts.
There are no verbs that exclude adverbs of location, merely some that
require them.)

   Handed in (4c) requires a noun phrase to its right, here *his wife*, and a
prepositional phrase describing a direction, here *into the carriage*. *Gave*
in (4d) allows the same types of complement as *handed*; 'allows' and not
'requires' because *gave* also occurs with two noun phrases as in (2c). Note
that not all verbs of giving or assigning behave like *give*. *Attribute* requires
the structure in (4d) but not the structure in (2c) – *Everyone attributed
good intentions to Frank Churchill* vs *Everyone attributed Frank Churchill good
intentions*. Finally, *suggested* in (5) is a verb that allows an ordinary noun
phrase to its right, as in *Mr Knightley suggested this plan*, but it also allows
a complement clause, here *that thieves would break into Hartfield House*.

Since very many verbs exclude a complement clause, the information that a complement clause is allowed must be stated in the dictionary entries for individual verbs.

5.3 Classes of verbs and subcategorisation restrictions

Some of these classes of verbs have traditional labels as listed in (6). These labels are convenient for talking about classes of verbs rather than individual verbs.

(6) *despair*   **Intransitive Verb** [excludes a noun phrase to its right, as in (2a)]

   slight   **Transitive Verb** [requires a noun phrase to its right, as in (2b)]

   gave   **Ditransitive Verb** ['twice transitive'] [requires two noun phrases to its right, as in (2c)]

   sat   **Intransitive Locational Verb** [excludes a noun phrase to its right but requires a prepositional phrase, as in (4a)]

   handed   **Transitive Directional Verb** [requires to its right both a noun phrase and a directional phrase]

   seemed   **Copula** (linking verb) [requires to its right an adjective phrase as in (3), or a noun phrase, as in *seemed a sensible person*, or a prepositional phrase, as in *seemed in good spirits*, or an infinitive, as in *seemed to be unhappy*]

To sum up, a given lexical item controls 'lexical insertion', the inserting of lexical items into its complements. Another approach that has been advocated more recently is to have no separate set of rules that specify syntactic structure but to have that work carried out by lexical entries. The entry for *seem* can be thought of as a set of instructions to build a syntactic structure containing a noun phrase, a verb and, for example, an adjective phrase. The entry for *hand* can be thought of as a set of instructions to build a syntactic structure containing a noun phrase, a verb, a noun phrase and a directional prepositional phrase, and so on for the other types of verb.

As well as controlling the number and general type of complements, lexical verbs control the choice of preposition. For example, *blame* occurs in the constructions in (7).

(7) a. Eleanor blamed Willoughby for Marianne's unhappiness.
    b. Eleanor blamed Marianne's unhappiness on Willoughby.

Depending on which way the event is presented, *blame* requires *for* or *on*;

no other prepositions are possible. Similarly, *accuse* requires the preposition *of*, as in *Eleanor accused Willoughby of unprincipled behaviour.*

The constraints that lexical verbs place on number and type of constituents, choice of preposition and choice of case are known as **subcategorisation**. We are dealing with the class or category of verbs, but the different constructions required by different verbs allow us to set up subclasses or subcategories of verb. Hence the term 'subcategorisation'. This discussion has not exhausted the topic of subcategorisation; in particular, we have not looked at combinations of plural verb and plural noun, singular verb and singular noun; or but we will take up this question in Chapter 9 on syntactic linkage.

5.4 Selectional restrictions

Lexical entries also contain information about the roles assigned to the nouns in a clause. (See Chapter 11 on participant roles.) For instance, *build* and *calculate* assign Agent role to their subject noun and Patient role to their direct object noun. In (8), *Romans* is Agent and *aqueduct* is Patient, and in (9) *computer* is Agent and *value* is Patient.

(8)   The Romans built this aqueduct.
(9)   The computer will calculate the value of the variable.

The fact that *aqueduct* is inanimate does not change the assignment of Patient role to it, and likewise the inanimacy of *computer* does not change the assignment of Agent role. Picking up from Chapter 4 the concept of the central, prototypical member of a class, we can say that prototypical Agents are animate, or even human. Inanimate nouns such as *computer* can be non-prototypical Agents, the role being thrust upon them by particular verbs and particular constructions. For instance, *calculate* requires an Agent, and in the ACTIVE DECLARATION construction the Agent role is assigned to the noun to the left of the verb.

Lexical verbs impose restrictions on the type of noun that can occur to their left or right. A verb such as *blame* requires a human noun to its left, while a verb such as *kill* requires an animate noun to its right. Of course, speakers and writers regularly utter sentences such as (10) and (11).

(10)   The dog blamed us for her stay at the vet's.
(11)   These objections killed the proposal.

Speakers and writers who produce (10) know perfectly well that blame is assigned by moral beings; they merely assume that dogs qualify. In our treatment of (11), we continue to state that *kill* requires an animate noun to its right. The clash between this requirement and the fact that *proposal* is inanimate imposes a metaphorical interpretation.

Constraints affecting the type of lexical noun are known as **selectional restrictions**. Selectional restrictions range from large classes of nouns such as animate and human nouns (shorthand for 'nouns denoting animate beings' and 'nouns denoting human beings') to smaller classes such as nouns denoting liquids. For example, the verb *flow* requires a subject noun such as *water*, *river* or *lava*, as in (12).

(12) The water/river flowed over the embankment

This particular verb raises two interesting points. The first is that, as with (10) and (11), the verb can be used metaphorically; we talk of ideas flowing from someone's pen. The second is that a given noun on its own may not denote a liquid but may be understood as doing so because of its modifiers. Thus *The molten metal flowed into the mould* does not require a metaphorical interpretation, but the fact that the metal is liquid is contributed by the adjective *molten*. This last example is handled in the same way as (11). Even without the adjective *molten*, it imposes the interpretation that the metal was in a liquid state and forces us to construct a suitable context, for example a foundry.

5.5 Classes of nouns

Selectional restrictions, as hinted above, lead us to employ large subclasses of nouns that are familiar from traditional grammar. The subclasses are set out in 13.

(13) a. **concrete** vs **abstract**
b. **common** vs **proper**
c. **count** vs **mass**
d. **animate** vs **inanimate**
e. **human** vs **non-human**

These subclasses were established in traditional grammar not just for the analysis of English but for the analysis of all the languages of Europe. They have been extended to the analysis of languages all over the world – many languages outside Europe have particularly intricate sets of distinctions. We have brought in these subclasses in connection with selectional restrictions, which are closely connected with semantics. A very important point, however, is that the distinctions set out in (13) are relevant to the grammar of many languages. We are not suggesting that all the distinctions are relevant to the grammar of every language, but any sample of languages from different language families and different areas of the world will show that each distinction affects the grammar of some languages. For example, English proper nouns such as *Ethel* typically exclude *the* and *a*, as discussed in Chapter 1 using the examples reproduced below as (14). Common nouns, which are not the names of people, towns and so on, typically allow or require *the* or *a*, for example *lecturer* in (14b), *gritter* and *salt* in (15a).

(14) a. Ethel was sitting at her desk.   *The Ethel was sitting at her desk.

    b. *Lecturer was sitting at her desk.   The lecturer was sitting at her desk.

(15) a. The gritter spread salt.   The gritter spread the salt.

    b. The gritter spread salts.

    c. Too much salt damages vehicles.   *Too many salt damages vehicles.

    d. *Too much vehicles are damaged by salt.   *Too many vehicles are damaged by salt.

The distinction between common and proper nouns does have a semantic component; proper nouns are the names of people, places, organisations and institutions. The distinction is also very important for the grammar of English noun phrases; proper nouns such as *Ethel* in (14a) exclude *the*, and singular common nouns such as *lecturer* in (14b) require *the*. (The plural does not – *Lecturers all wear food-stained pullovers and sandals* is impeccable in its grammar even if not in its content.)

The distinction between count and mass nouns is involved in important grammatical choices but likewise has a meaning component. With respect to grammar, mass nouns require *much*, as in (15c), and exclude *many*; count nouns require *many* and exclude *much*. With respect to meaning, count nouns refer to entities that are thought of as individuals, that can be counted – boy, plant, idea. Mass nouns denote entities that are conceived of as a mass of stuff that cannot be split into countable individuals – water, flour, wine, salt. Mass nouns typically occur in the singular; when they occur in the plural, they change their meaning. *Wines* has the interpretation 'kinds of wine'.

In other languages, the distinctions between the subclasses of nouns are relevant for the assignment of case, for example. This is demonstrated by the two Russian examples in (16).

(16) a. Boris podnjal   stakan
      Boris picked-up   (the)-glass

    b. Boris podnjal   kota
      Boris picked-up   (the)-cat [tomcat]

Stakan in (16a) is inanimate and has no case suffix. *Kot* is animate and takes the case suffix *-a*. Other patterns in the Russian case system involve the distinction between concrete and abstract and between count and mass, but we omit the details.

We close this section with a comment on the terms 'concrete' and 'abstract'. *Lecturer* and *wine* are examples of concrete nouns, while *truth* and *amazement* are abstract nouns. We are using the traditional labels, but the key distinction is whether a given noun denotes an entity that is abstract or not abstract. The difficulty is that 'concrete' evokes an entity made of the substance called 'concrete', or at least an entity that is hard and solid. Lecturers are not made of the substance we call 'concrete' and wine is not solid, but neither wine nor lecturers are abstract. They can be physically seen, touched and manipulated, whereas truth and amazement cannot.

5.6 Subcategorisation, selection and constructions

The last comment in connection with subclasses of nouns is that labels such as 'concrete', 'count' and 'human' represent properties of nouns; these properties are known as inherent properties, and features such as 'concrete' are known as inherent features.

All the examples in this chapter have been of the ACTIVE DECLARATIVE construction, that is, of the basic construction as defined in Chapter 3. As discussed there, the construction of an example such as (2c) is related to a number of other constructions, as shown in (17).

(17) a. Frank Churchill gave a piano to Jane Fairfax.
      b. Frank Churchill gave Jane Fairfax a piano.
      c. A piano was given to Jane Fairfax by Frank Churchill.

Let us say for the sake of the argument that in the ACTIVE DECLARATIVE construction *give* requires an animate noun to its left referring to the giver, *Frank Churchill*, and a prepositional phrase to its right, also containing an animate noun but referring to the recipient, *to Jane Fairfax*. Example (17b) is an example of the ditransitive construction; the same lexical items occur, but the animate noun *Jane Fairfax* is a noun phrase immediately following the verb and not preceded by a preposition. In (17c), an example of the passive construction, the animate noun *Frank Churchill* is not to the left of the verb but to its right, inside a prepositional phrase, *by Frank Churchill*.

We could write separate dictionary entries for *give* for all three constructions, but this has two drawbacks. We would have to write separate entries for each construction that a given verb occurs in, and there are many different constructions. More seriously, we would not capture in our account the system of constructions, the fact that paths lead from the basic ACTIVE DECLARATIVE positive construction out to the other constructions, some directly, some via intervening constructions. (See the discussion in Chapter 3.) The way round this problem is to state the subcategorisation and selectional restrictions once for the basic ACTIVE DECLARATIVE positive construction and to have the information about the restrictions carried from one construction to the next. (The details of the transfer from one construction to another differ from one model to another, and it is no easy task to state the details explicitly; nonetheless, what has been stated above is the goal shared by all the models of syntax.)

5.7 Fixed phrases

We round off this brief visit to the dictionary by pointing out that we began with the stereotypical view that there are rules that specify syntactic constructions and that words are listed in the dictionary or lexicon, taken out of the dictionary and inserted into syntactic constructions. It turned out that the connection between syntax and lexical items is closer than we might have imagined, not only with respect to the number of connections but also with respect to the powerful role played by individual lexical items, especially verbs. Over the past fifteen years or so, analysts have come to realise that in any language there is a large set of phrases and even whole clauses that are not freely built up but fixed. Following the discussion by Crystal in *The Cambridge Encyclopaedia of the English Language* (pp. 162–3), we can distinguish various types of fixed phrase, as set out in (18)–(21).

(18) POLYWORDS: in a nutshell; once and for all

(19) INSTITUTIONALISED EXPRESSIONS: Give me a break; How do you do?; Long time no see; Pleased to meet you; See you soon; come to think of it; it doesn't bear thinking about

(20) HIGHLY CONSTRAINED PHRASES: as I was __ (saying/ mentioning); as far as I __ (can see/can make out/know); I (just) can't think straight; I thought I told you not to do that

(21) SENTENCE BUILDERS: my point is that __; let me begin by ___; not only … but also

Crystal also discusses collocations, restricted sequences of words; examples are in (22). *Heavy smoker* and *heavy drinker* qualify as collocations because *heavy* and *light* combine with a limited set of nouns – *smoker*, *drinker*, *eater* and *sleeper*.

(22) COLLOCATIONS: staple food/diet/industry; wouldn't/won't/
couldn't budge; a heavy smoker; a heavy drinker

The above five types of phrase and clause do not always conform to the syntax of written English and may have idiosyncratic meanings; a heavy smoker is not a smoker with a weight problem. It looks as though these phrases and clauses must be listed as single items in the dictionary, although at the time of writing there are no explicit descriptions of English or other languages that handle fixed phrases in an adequate way. What analysts are more and more certain of is that the number of fixed expressions in English (and other languages) and the frequency with which they are used by speakers and writers is much greater than anyone supposed forty years ago.

Summary

The traditional view of clauses and sentences is that syntactic structures, like those in Appendix 2, are built up and that lexical items are inserted into the structures, again as shown in the diagrams in Appendix 2. In fact, lexical items can be seen as playing an important and even controlling role. For instance, *blame* requires a noun phrase to its right, *Emma blamed Harriet*, and while it does not require a prepositional phrase it allows one and requires the preposition to be *for* – *Emma blamed Harriet for the mistake*. Some verbs, such as *disappear*, exclude any noun phrase to their right; witness **The magician disappeared the investment funds*. Other verbs exclude entire constructions; *resemble* excludes the passive, and **Your friend is resembled by my brother* is unacceptable. Particular verbs require particular types of noun to their left or right; *faint* requires an animate noun to its left, as in *The patient fainted* vs **The engine fainted*, and *persuade* requires an animate noun to its right, as in *We persuaded the students (to write their essays)* vs **We persuaded the lava (to flow into the lake)*. Verbs are said to select particular types of noun and to impose selectional restrictions. Verbs can be divided into subcategories with respect to the number and type of phrases they require, exclude or allow. The phenomenon is known as subcategorisation, and verbs are said to subcategorise for particular types of constituents.

Exercises

1. In (6) above, various classes of verb are exemplified – intransitive, transitive, ditransitive, intransitive locational, transitive directional and copula. Which class does each of the following verbs belong to?

BECOME ANTAGONISE FIND HANG SUSPEND SEND LOCK TURN

2. A special class of modal verbs is recognised in English. *Can* is one of them. On the basis of the following examples, say what properties distinguish modal verbs from ordinary verbs.

   1. The firm can deliver the documents to your house.
   2. The firm can't/cannot deliver the documents before Friday.
   3. The firm delivers the documents to your house.
   4. The firm doesn't/does not deliver the documents to your house.
   5. Can the firm deliver the documents to my house?
   6. Does the firm can deliver documents to my house?
   7. The firm can deliver the documents to my house, can't it?
   8. The firm delivers the document to your house, doesn't it?
   9. I emphasise that the firm *can* deliver documents to your house.
   10. I emphasise that the firm *does* deliver documents to your house.
   11. At the moment, the firm is delivering documents inside twenty-four hours.
   12. *At the moment the firm is canning (= is able to) deliver documents inside twenty-four hours

3. Is *ought* a modal verb for speakers who produce examples such as (4) and (5) below? Do you use the constructions in (1), (2) and (3)? In speech or in writing or both?

   1. Ought he to leave his luggage lying there?
   2. Oughtn't you to be working for the examinations?
   3. We oughtn't to be helping them.
   4. They ought to pay attention to these arguments, didn't they?
   5. You didn't ought to listen to them.

Is *need* a modal verb for speakers who produce examples such as (6)–(8) below? Do you speak or write examples such as (9)–(11)?

   6. You're needing to have a haircut.
   7. Do they need to be paid the whole sum at once?
   8. They don't need to sit this examination.
   9. Need we take this examination?
   10. They needn't sit this examination.
   11. You need to have a haircut.

4. In (13) above, various classes of nouns were set up and assigned inherent features: animate vs inanimate, concrete vs abstract, count vs mass, common vs proper, human vs non-human. Which of these features can be assigned to the following nouns?

   CANADA   WINE   MOUSE   TRUTH   RUMOUR   GLASS   GRANT

Take the following examples into account.

1. The mouse ran under the desk.
2. I always use the mouse to move the cursor.
3. How much wine has he drunk?
4. This shop specialises in Australian wines.
5. She always told the truth, no matter the consequences.
6. She told him a few home truths about himself.
7. Some nasty rumours are going about.
8. Rumour has it that she is being promoted.
9. When did the Venetians discover how to make fine glass?
10. We only have ten glasses for twelve people.
11. I only wear my glasses when reading.
12. She was given a grant for her research.
13. How many grants does the council award each year?
14. How much grant does the university receive?

6 Clauses I

6.1 Clauses and sentences

We have discussed dependency relations (heads and modifiers), constituent structure (the arrangements of words into phrases and phrases into clauses) and constructions. Key technical terms such as 'clause' and 'sentence' have been used without any attempt at definition, but it is now time to take up this task. It is also an appropriate point at which to discuss the central concepts of **'main clause'** and **'subordinate clause'**; without them, we cannot discuss in any insightful way the organisation of clauses into the sentences which make up effective written texts. ('Written texts', because the syntax and textual organisation of spontaneous speech is rather different.) We can usefully begin by reviewing the major properties of clauses, taking the examples in (1) as our starting point.

(1) a. Wickham eloped with Lydia.
     b. Miss Bates chattered on for hours.

Examples (1a, b) are sentences. It is hard to supply an instant definition of a sentence apart from the initial capital letter and the final full stop, but we will return to sentences later in the chapter. Examples (1a, b) are also instances of main clauses. What are the major properties of these main clauses?

i   Each clause contains a finite verb; that is, a verb marked for tense. (For further remarks on the notion of 'finiteness' and the concept of non-finite clause, see Chapter 7.) **Finite verbs** are traditionally said to be marked for tense, person and number. **Tense** has to do with whether the speaker or writer uses a past-tense verb, for example *was* in *was listening*, and places a given event in past time, or a present-tense verb, for example *is* in *is listening*, and places the event in present time. **Person** has to do with whether an action is assigned to the speaker (*I am listening*, first person), the hearer (*You are listening*, second person) or someone other than the speaker and hearer (*He/she is listening*, third person). **Number** has to do with whether the speaker or writer refers to one person (*She is listening*, singular) or more than one (*They are listening*, plural).

Person and number are mostly lacking in English verbs with the exception of BE, which has a first person singular form *am*, a third person singular form *is*, and the form *are* for the plural and the second person. In the past tense (see the discussion of tense in Chapter 13), it has the form *was* for the first and third person singular and the form *were* for the plural and the second person. (Other languages have a richer system of person and number contrasts, as in the Russian *chitaem Solzhenitsyna* 'we are reading Solzhenitsyn', *chitaju Solzhenitsyna* 'I am reading Solzhenitsyn', *chitaesh' Solzhenitsyna* 'you are reading Solzhenitsyn', and so on. The suffix *-em* signals first person, plural and present tense; *-ju* signals first person, singular and present tense, and *-esh'* signals second person, singular and present tense.)

ii   In each clause, the finite verb is accompanied by its complements and adjuncts (see Chapter 1).

iii   Each clause is marked for **aspect** (see Chapter 13), and the aspect can be changed: compare *Wickham was eloping with Lydia* as opposed to *Wickham eloped with Lydia*.

iv   Each clause has mood. Mood has to do with two sets of distinctions. First, there are the distinctions between making statements (*Wickham eloped with Lydia*), asking questions (*Did Wickham elope with Lydia?*) (see Chapter 13) and issuing commands (*Elope with Lydia!*). The second set of distinctions has to do with whether the speaker or writer presents an event as possible (*He may have eloped with Lydia*) or as necessary (*He must have eloped with Lydia*) or as a fact (*He did elope with Lydia.*) (See Chapter 13 for further discussion.)

v   Both allow certain changes of syntax to reflect changes of focus or emphasis, for example *Never will Wickham elope with Lydia*, *With Lydia Wickham eloped (to London)*, *Eloped with Lydia to London*, *Wickham did* (colloquial but relevant).

vi   Clauses describe situations, the participants in them (for example, Agents carrying out actions on Patients, as in *Frank* [Agent] *persuaded Jane* [Patient] *to keep the secret*, and the circumstances in which they take place, as in *Frank Churchill was in Hartfield* [place] *in June* [time]). (The term 'circumstances' may seem strange but is a technical term which now has a long history.)

vii   Both can be the first contribution to a discourse, whether spoken or written. Clearly, this rests on presuppositions about the audience knowing who Wickham, Lydia and so on are, but what is important for present purposes is that phrases such as *with Lydia*, *handed his hat to the servant* and *chattered on* cannot be the first contribution to a normal

English text, nor can clauses such as *which she bought last week* or *although it is cold*. Of course these phrases and clauses occur in texts, but not as the first contribution. The phrases can only be responses, as in *Who did Wickham elope with? – with Lydia*, or just *Lydia*, and clauses such as *although it is cold* must be combined with main clauses.

The central fact in the above list is that we can recognise clauses by which phrases modify ('go with') which verb; that is, we can recognise clauses in real texts – novels, newspapers, poems, academic textbooks and even the transcripts of conversation. What we are doing here is introducing the clause as part of our analysis, and it will be useful to have different labels for the two sorts of clause. Clauses in real texts we will call '**text clauses**'; clauses in our analysis we will call '**system clauses**', capturing the fact that in our analysis we try to establish a system of grammar, and clauses are part of the system.

We need the clause for a coherent description of dependency relations (including agreement and government, as discussed in Chapters 8 and 9) and constituent structure. The densest clusters of dependency relations are found inside clauses (although some dependency relations do reach from one clause to another, as in the occurrence of *which* or *who* in relative clauses; which one occurs depends on a noun outside the relative clause – *the book which* but *the woman who*). The tests for constituent structure work best inside single clauses. Fortunately, the clauses that are part of our analysis typically correspond to clauses in real texts. The unit that does cause problems, surprisingly, is the sentence.

6.2 Main and subordinate clauses

Writers, whether novelists or people writing personal letters to family and friends, put clauses together into sentences, and it is for this activity that main clauses and the different types of subordinate clause are essential. Some sentences in texts (**text sentences**, corresponding to text clauses) resemble the examples in (1) in consisting of a single main clause, but many consist of several clauses. Depending on what types of clause are combined, two types of multi-clause sentence are distinguished. **Compound sentences** consist of two or more clauses joined by conjunctions. Examples are given in (2).

(2) a. Captain Benwick married Louisa Hayter and Captain Wentworth married Anne Elliott.
   b. Henry Crawford loved Fanny but Fanny loved Edmund.
   c. Mr Bingley became tired of Jane or Mr D'Arcy persuaded Mr Bingley to go to London.

In (2a), the clauses *Captain Benwick married Louisa Hayter* and *Captain Wentworth married Anne Elliott* are conjoined by *and*; in (2b) the clauses *Henry Crawford loved Fanny* and *Fanny loved Edmund* are conjoined by *but*; and in (2c) the clauses *Mr Bingley became tired of Jane* and *Mr D'Arcy persuaded Mr Bingley to go to London* are conjoined by *or*. In (2a–c), the conjoined clauses are all main clauses, but subordinate clauses can also be conjoined, as we will see after the following discussion of subordinate clauses.

6.3 Subordinate clauses

Complex sentences consist of a main clause and one or more other clauses subordinate to it. That is, one clause, the main clause, is pre-eminent in a complex sentence and the other clauses, the subordinate clauses, are subject to certain limitations, as will be shown later. We begin by giving examples of the major types of subordinate clause, complement clause, relative clause and adverbial clause.

6.3.1 Complement clauses

Examples of complement clauses are given in (3a, b).

(3) a. Elizabeth regretted *that she had met Wickham.*
    b. Catherine feared *that the Abbey was haunted.*

These clauses were traditionally called 'noun clauses', because they occur in slots in the main clause that can be occupied by ordinary noun phrases – *Elizabeth regretted her actions* and *Catherine feared the General's temper.* The contemporary label 'complement clause' reflects the relationship between the clauses and the verb of the main clause: *Elizabeth regretted* and *Catherine feared* are incomplete pieces of syntax which require a modifier, either a noun phrase as in the immediately preceding examples or a clause, as in (3).

The complement clauses in (3) occur to the right of the verbs in the main clauses, but complement clauses also occur to the left of verbs, as in (4).

(4) *That Anne was in conversation with Mr Elliott* dismayed Captain Wentworth.

The skeleton of the sentence in (4) is *[   ] dismayed Captain Wentworth*, the square brackets marking the slot waiting for some constituent. The slot could be filled by a noun phrase such as *Her words* but in (4) is filled by the complement clause *That Anne was in conversation with Mr Elliott.*

There is one more property of complement clauses to be mentioned here; they can modify a noun, as in (5).

(5) Fanny was delighted by the idea *that she could subscribe to a library.*

The sequence *Fanny was delighted by the idea* is a complete clause. The additional *that she could subscribe to a library* conveys the content of the idea. It is not required to complete the syntax, but as we will see later it is not a relative clause and has been given the label 'complement clause' because it fills out the meaning of the word *idea.* Other examples of noun complement clauses are given in (6), *that the committee be abolished* and *that we would visit Glasgow today.*

(6) a. Who thought up the proposal *that the committee be abolished*?
     b. There was a plan *that we would visit Glasgow today* but the weather is terrible.

6.3.2 Relative clauses

Complement clauses modify verbs as in (3) and (4) and nouns as in (6); relative clauses modify nouns. In older descriptions, relative clauses are called adjective clauses, reflecting the fact that adjectives also modify nouns. Of course, in English they do not occur in the same position as adjectives, since adjectives typically precede the noun in a noun phrase while relative clauses follow it. Examples of relative clauses are given in (7).

(7) a. The cottage *which Mrs Dashwood accepted* was rather small.
     b. The gentleman *who saved Marianne* was Willoughby.
     c. The book *which Marianne was reading* contained poems by Cowper.
     d. The building *that we liked* is in Thornton Lacey.

In (7a), the relative clause *which Mrs Dashwood accepted* modifies the noun *cottage*; in (7b) the relative clause *who saved Marianne* modifies the noun *gentleman*; in (7c) the relative clause *which Marianne was reading* modifies the noun *book*; and in (7d) the relative clause *that we liked* modifies the noun *building.* In certain circumstances, the WH word or *that* can be omitted, as in *The building we liked is in Thornton Lacey*, with the relative clause *we liked*, or *The book Marianne was reading contained poems by Cowper*, with the relative clause *Marianne was reading.*

(The term 'relative' goes back to the Roman grammarians, who called the Latin equivalent of *which, who* and so on relative pronouns because they referred back to a noun. *Refer* derives from the Latin verb *referre*, a very irregular verb whose past participle passive is *relatus*, from which 'related' derives. Note that although the *that* clause in (7d) is called a relative clause, *that* is not a relative pronoun but a conjunction.)

6.3.3 Adverbial clauses

The name 'adverbial' suggests that adverbial clauses modify verbs; but they modify whole clauses, as shown by the examples in (8). Their other key property is that they are adjuncts, since they are typically optional constituents in sentences. They are traditionally classified according to their meaning, for example adverbial clauses of reason, time, concession, manner or condition, as illustrated below.

(8) a. **Reason**
   Because Marianne loved Willoughby, she refused to believe that he had deserted her.
   b. **Time**
   When Fanny returned, she found Tom Bertram very ill.
   c. **Concession**
   Although Mr D'Arcy disliked Mrs Bennet he married Elizabeth.
   d. **Manner**
   Henry changed his plans *as the mood took him*.
   e. **Condition**
   If Emma had left Hartfield, Mr Woodhouse would have been unhappy.

The adverbial clause of reason in (8a), *Because Marianne loved Willoughby*, gives the reason (or the writer uses it to give the reason) why Marianne refused to believe that Willoughby had gone. It modifies the main clause *she refused to believe that he had deserted her.*

The adverbial clause of time in (8b), *When Fanny returned*, gives the time at which another event happened, namely her finding Tom Bertram ill. It modifies the main clause *she found Tom Bertram very ill.*

The adverbial clause of concession in (8c), *Although Mr D'Arcy disliked Mrs Bennet*, conveys a concession. The writer says, as it were, 'OK. I concede that he didn't like Mrs Bennet. Nonetheless he married Elizabeth.' The adverbial clause modifies the main clause *he married Elizabeth.*

The adverbial clause of manner in (8d), *as the mood took him*, describes the manner in which Henry changed his plans and modifies the main clause *Henry changed his plans.*

In (8e), the adverbial clause of condition *If Emma had left Hartfield* conveys the circumstances or conditions under which a particular situation would have arisen. The situation is Mr Woodhouse being unhappy, and the writer declares that this situation did not actually come about but would have done; Emma's leaving Hartfield would have brought it about. The crucial fact is the relationship between the two situations; Mr Woodhouse's being unhappy is conditional upon Emma's leaving Hartfield. The adverbial clause of condition modifies the main clause *Mr Woodhouse would have been unhappy*.

6.4 Complementisers and subordinating conjunctions

One important point remains to be made about subordinate clauses (in English). Most of the subordinate clauses you will come across in written texts are introduced by a special word. In (3), the complement clauses are introduced by *that*, in (7) the relative clauses are introduced by *which*, *who* and *that*, and in (8) each type of adverbial clause has its particular initial word, *although*, *because*, *as*, *when* and *if*. In grammars from before, say, 1965, the words introducing complement clauses and adverbial clauses were generally known as **subordinating conjunctions**, and words such as *and* or *but* were known as **coordinating conjunctions**. Conjunctions are words that (con)join clauses. Coordinating conjunctions join clauses that have the same status. In (2a), for example, the clause *Captain Benwick married Louisa Hayter* is of the same status as *Captain Wentworth married Anne Elliott*. If (2a) were split into its component clauses, each clause on its own would immediately be able to constitute a sentence and to occur in a text. The clauses are of the same order or rank, hence **co**-ordinating conjunction and **co**-ordinate clauses.

In contrast, if (8e), say, were split into its component clauses, only one of them would be able to constitute a sentence, namely the main clause *Mr Woodhouse would have been unhappy*. The adverbial clause of condition, *if Emma had left Hartfield*, cannot function as a sentence until the subordinating conjunction *if* is removed. Subordinating conjunctions introduce subordinate clauses. Since 1965 or so, the term 'complementiser' has been used in one of the major theories of syntax not just for subordinating conjunctions introducing complement clauses but for all subordinating conjunctions. This usage has spread to other theories of syntax and to grammars of English and other languages, and we too adopt it.

A problem is posed by the words that introduce relative clauses. *Who*, *whom* and *which* are pronouns that also function as subordinating conjunctions. That they are pronouns is indicated by the *who/whom* distinction parallel to *he/him* and so on and the contrast between *who* and *which*, parallel to the contrast between *he/she* and *it*. (The contrast between *who* and *whom* is disappearing from English. It is only used regularly in the most formal and carefully edited texts.) The WH words can be preceded by prepositions, as in *the fire at which Mr Woodhouse sat*. The WH words will sometimes be referred to as **relative pronouns** and sometimes as complementisers. Relative clauses are also introduced by *that*. This word does not change (in technical terms, is invariable) and cannot be preceded by a preposition – **the fire at that Mr Woodhouse sat*. It is not a pronoun but merely a subordinating conjunction or complementiser.

All the subordinate clauses in (8) are optional and can occur no matter what verb is in the main clause. For this reason, they are treated as adjuncts. The above list of adverbial clauses is not exhaustive but merely illustrative. Detailed accounts of subordinate clauses in English and other languages can be found in the references at the end of the book.

To close this section, we return to conjoined clauses. Examples of conjoined main clauses were given in (2), but subordinate clauses can also be conjoined, as shown by the examples in (9). Example (9a) contains two conditional clauses conjoined by *and*; (9b) contains two relative clauses conjoined by *but*.

(9) a. If Henry Crawford loved Fanny and if Fanny loved Edward, Henry Crawford was going to be disappointed.
     b. It was Anne Elliott who loved Captain Wentworth but who rejected his first proposal.

6.5 Recognising clauses

There are reliable rules of thumb for recognising the different types of clause. Some of the rules have to do with constituent structure or the complementiser, but most of them exploit the concept of modification.

Rules of thumb

For any given finite subordinate clause:

A Does it modify another clause? If it does, it is an **ADVERBIAL CLAUSE**.

For example, in (10) the clause in italics modifies the entire clause in roman type. It establishes a time for the entire situation of leaving the furniture behind and is an adverbial clause of time.

(10) *When we sell the house*, we'll probably leave most of the furniture.

B Does it modify a verb? If it does, it is a **(VERB) COMPLEMENT CLAUSE**.

For example, in (11) the clause in italics modifies the verb *reported*. Indeed, the clause *A motorist has reported* is incomplete without the complement clause.

(11)   A motorist has reported *that the road is blocked by snow at Soutra Hill.*

NB: Verb complement clauses function as subject or object of a clause.

C   Does it modify a noun? If it does, it could be a **RELATIVE CLAUSE** or a **COMPLEMENT CLAUSE**.

C(i)   Is the subordinate clause introduced by a WH word such as *who, which, where,* or by a prepositional phrase such as *in which*? If it is, it is a relative clause.

For example, in (12) and (13) the clauses in italics are relative clauses.

(12)   The Labrador ate all the food *which we left on the kitchen table.*

(13)   Show me the folder *in which you stored the documents.*

C(ii)   Is the subordinate clause introduced by *that*? If it is, it could be either a relative clause or a complement clause. If it is a relative clause, *that* can be replaced by *which* and so on, as in (14). If it is a complement clause, *that* cannot be replaced by a WH word, as shown by (15).

(14)   **RELATIVE CLAUSE**
        a. I like the book *that you gave me.*
        b. I like the book *which you gave me.*

(15)   **COMPLEMENT CLAUSE**
        a. We like the idea *that the city centre will be pedestrianised.*
        b. *We like the idea *which the city centre will be pedestrianised.*

Note that there are some examples that go counter to **C(ii)**. In *the question why she bothered phoning, the reason why they refused* and *the problem where to leave our furniture,* the nouns *question, reason* and *problem* are followed by WH clauses, but these clauses are complements. Other, more formal, variants are *the question of why she bothered phoning* and *the problem of where to leave our furniture.* In the latter examples the nouns *question* and *problem* are linked to the WH clause by the preposition *of.* Relative clauses are never linked to nouns in this way. We will treat these apparent counter-examples as fixed phrases, since a very limited number of nouns are modified by WH complement clauses.

There is a further useful test that distinguishes between relative and noun complement clauses. Consider the verb complement clause above and in (3) and all the adverbial clauses we have looked at. If you remove the complementiser, you are left with a complete clause; the removal of *that* from *that she had met Wickham* in (3a) leaves *she had met Wickham*, and the removal of *Although* from *Although Mr D'Arcy disliked Mrs Bennet* in (8c) leaves *Mr D'Arcy disliked Mrs Bennet*. The removal of *that* from the noun complement clause *that she could subscribe to a library* in (5) leaves *she could subscribe to a library*.

Removal of the complementiser from relative clauses produces a different result. In (7a), the removal of *which* from *which Mrs Dashwood accepted* leaves *Mrs Dashwood accepted*. This is not a complete clause, since *accepted* requires a noun phrase to its right. The removal of *who* from *who saved Marianne* in (7b) leaves *saved Marianne*. This clause is incomplete because the verb requires a noun to its left. It makes no difference whether a given relative clause is introduced by a WH word or *that*, as in (7d). The removal of *that* in the latter leaves *we liked*, which lacks a noun phrase to its right and is incomplete.

6.6 Final comment

In the above examples, the relative and complement clauses are introduced by *that*, *who* and *which*. Relative and complement clauses often follow their head noun or verb directly, without a complementiser, as in (16).

(16)   a.   I love the food *they cook in the halls of residence.*
       b.   A motorist has reported *the road is blocked at Soutra Hill.*
       c.   I am delighted at the idea *they might demolish the Appleton Tower.*

The lack of a complementiser does not affect the rules of thumb. Example (16b) contains a verb complement clause, *the road is blocked at Soutra Hill*, which modifies *reported*; (16a) contains a relative clause, *they cook in the halls of residence*, modifying *food*; and (16c) contains a complement clause, *they might demolish the Appleton Tower*, modifying the noun *idea*.

Summary

Three major types of subordinate clause are recognised: complement clauses, relative clauses and adverbial clauses. Complement clauses modify either verbs or nouns, can function as subject or object in a clause and have as their complementiser *that* or zero. Relative clauses modify nouns and have as their complementiser a WH word or *that* or zero. Relative clauses differ further from complement clauses in that, without a WH complementiser, they lack a subject or object. This also applies to relative clauses introduced by *that* or zero. Adverbial clauses modify other clauses. Rules of thumb based largely on modification help to pick out the different types of clause.

Exercises

The following exercises contain sentences consisting of two or more clauses. Analyse each sentence into its clauses and state the type of each clause – main clause, adverbial clause (of reason, concession and so on), relative clause, complement clause. The examples in Exercises 1–3 are either made up or adapted from 'real' sentences. The examples in Exercise 4 are from a magazine article.

1. 1. Jane believes that the earrings she got from Susan are real silver.
    2. I'll believe it when I see it.
    3. If you think Scotland are ever going to win the European Championship, you must be a real optimist.
    4. The article in which the theory was put forward is now unobtainable.
    5. That Helen is to marry the man she met on holiday has surprised all her friends.
    6. Celia did not say that you could keep the book that you borrowed.
    7. Because you are flying non-stop, you will probably have severe jet-lag.
    8. He promised that he would be here on time, though I find it difficult to rely on him.
    9. The woman whose car you think you have dented is our MP.
    10. That you don't like my home-made vodka I find difficult to believe.
    11. Since you think you are ready to sit the test, come along tomorrow.
    12. That the club regained the trophy dismayed the teams that had better players.

2. 1. We regret that the plan is impracticable.
    2. They accept the theory that the world is flat.
    3. They accept the theory that the group proposed.
    4. Did Fiona say who would be at the party?
    5. Which of the candidates will be elected is quite unpredictable.
    6. It is believed by some historians that Napoleon was poisoned.

3. 1. Kirsty went out and forgot to switch off the gas fire.

2. We know that she wrote several novels and threw them away.

3. The editors who ignored the ban and printed the story might find themselves in prison.

4. If you go walking on the hills in winter and do not take proper equipment, you are asking for trouble.

4. 1. They are pioneering a new geography in which they will establish when new races settled in particular regions.

   2. A geneticist says the Pacific islands are an ideal testing ground for the theory that the Pacific was colonised from west to east.

   3. The history begins with the day when the chief medical officer for Vanuatu noticed that a large number of people there suffered from anaemia.

   4. He was advised to treat them with iron supplements so he contacted scientists at Oxford who found that half of the donors suffered from alpha-thalassaemia, which is usually linked to the presence of malaria.

   5. It seems that the gene protects against malaria, since carriers of the alpha 3.7 mutant will not die of malaria even if they contract a severe bout.

   6. Although anthropological studies have been inconclusive, previous biological research has suggested that there was no contact while the Melanesians were moving east.

7 Clauses II

Chapter 6 dealt with the basic properties of main and subordinate clauses. In this chapter, we will discuss further topics – the relationship between main and subordinate clauses, the characteristics of subordinate clauses and the question of non-finite clauses.

7.1 Main and subordinate clauses

One very traditional view of subordinate clauses is that they derive from main clauses which are put into subordinate positions in sentences and undergo certain syntactic changes. In many languages other than English, they also undergo morphological changes, since a given verb turns up in one shape in main clauses and another shape in (particular types of) subordinate clause. This is easily demonstrated via the French *elle peut* 'she can [main clause]' and *afin qu'elle puisse* 'so that she can [subordinate clause, an adverbial clause of purpose]', where only *puisse* occurs in adverbial clauses of purpose and only *peut* occurs in main clauses.

The relationship between main and subordinate clauses was foreshadowed in the discussion of rules of thumb at the end of the previous chapter. There, we saw that when a complementiser is removed from an adverbial clause or a complement clause in English it leaves a sequence of words which make up a complete main clause. The removal of the complementiser from relative clauses, however, leaves a sequence that lacks either the noun phrase which would be to the left of the verb or the noun phrase which would be to the right of the verb. A second complication is that WH words seem to be both pronouns and complementisers, whereas *that* is purely a complementiser.

One way of handling the relationship is to assume that the route from main clause to relative clause is as follows, taking (7a) in Chapter 6 as our example, repeated here as (1).

(1) The cottage which Mrs Dashwood accepted was very small.

Assume that the source of the relative clause *which Mrs Dashwood accepted* is *Mrs Dashwood accepted which*, with the pronoun *which* in the usual slot for direct objects. The pronoun *which* is moved to the front of the clause, in fact to a special slot for complementisers outside the main body of the clause. This enables us to show both that *which* is the direct object of *accepted* and that it is the complementiser of the relative clause. (This treatment appeals to the idea introduced in Chapter 3 on constructions: they can be thought of as arranged in a network with specific paths through the network from construction to construction. In that chapter, we looked only at main clauses, but the idea is here extended to the relationship between main and subordinate clauses.) The analysis of relative clauses can be made more complex if we take at its face value the definition of pronouns as substituting for nouns – more accurately, for noun phrases. One line of analysis would take the source of the above relative clause to be *Mrs Dashwood accepted the cottage*, with *which* being substituted for *the cottage* and then being moved to the complementiser slot.

Relative clauses with the complementiser *that* have a different source. Since *that* is not a pronoun, there is no reason to start with it in subject or object position and then move it. In the source main clause, it is in the complementiser slot. But in the source main clause, *accepted* needs an object. We solve this problem by assuming that the source main clause is *that Mrs Dashwood accepted it*. En route to the relative clause, *it* is dropped.

We have space to discuss only one simple example. Anyone who takes further this sort of analysis quickly finds that the details of even short examples are not straightforward. Furthermore, the analysis sketched above is fairly superficial; attempts to gain depth inevitably lead to analyses that are both very detailed and very abstract. One final point in this section: as was said in Chapter 3 on constructions, it is tempting to think of moving backwards and forwards along the paths through the network of constructions, and it is equally tempting to think of being able to move from main clause to subordinate clause or vice versa. In practice, all recent detailed analyses of syntax of this type specify paths from a source construction, a starting point, out through the network to more complex constructions, and not in the opposite direction.

7.2 Clause and sentence

We noted in Chapters 1, 2 and 6 that the clause is an important unit of analysis because many head–modifier relations are found within the clause and because the criteria for constituent structure, such as transposition, apply best inside the clause. The sentence is not very useful in these respects; only a few dependency relations cross clause boundaries, and the constituent structure criteria do not really apply outside single clauses. Consider (2a–b).

(2) a. Anne Musgrave has just seen Mr Elliott in Bath Street.
   b. Nurse Rooke has discovered where Anne Elliott stayed.
   c. Nurse Rooke suspected that Mrs Clay planned to run away with Mr Elliott.

Example (2a) contains a single main clause, which can stand on its own and constitute a sentence. Within that clause, there is a relatively dense network of dependencies. (*Has*) *seen* has the two NPs as complements – it requires both a noun phrase to its left and a noun phrase to its right. The form of HAVE must be *has* and not *have*, since there is agreement in number between the first noun phrase and the verb. If we replace *Mr Elliott* with a pronoun, the pronoun has to be *him* and not *he*. The Perfect, *has seen*, allows time adverbs such as *just* but excludes time adverbs such as *in March* or *five years ago*.

Example (2b) contains the main clause *Nurse Rooke has discovered where Anne Elliott stayed.* The object of *discovered* is itself a clause, *where Anne Elliott stayed.* This complement clause is said to be embedded in the main clause and is controlled by *discovered*. Only some verbs allow a clause as opposed to an ordinary noun phrase, and DISCOVER is one of them. Of the verbs that allow complement clauses, only some allow WH complementisers such as *where*, and DISCOVER is one of them. Like DISCOVER, PLAN allows complement clauses (*We planned that they would only stay for two nights – but alas …*), but also infinitives, as in (2c); SUSPECT on the other hand excludes infinitives.

It is generally accepted that we can specify where words occur in phrases, and where phrases occur in clauses, but not where entire sentences occur in a text. This does not mean that the sentences in a text are devoid of links. Sentences in a paragraph can be linked by binders such as *thus, in other words, for this reason, consequently, nevertheless*, or by the ellipsis of certain portions of a sentence that depend on the preceding sentences in a discourse – *I can help you tomorrow. Sheila can't [help you tomorrow]*; and by pronouns – *Kerry and Louise have failed the maths exam. Margaret and Sheila are not pleased with them.* The links between sentences in texts are different from the dependencies between the constituents in clauses, being less predictable and more flexible.

We can say something about where clauses occur in sentences. Relative clauses are embedded in noun phrases and immediately follow the head noun. (But not always, as in the well-used example *I got a jug from India that was broken.*) Verb complement clauses substitute for either noun phrase with a transitive verb. *Anne* in (3a) is replaced in (3b) by the

complement clause *That Captain Wentworth married Anne. The scene* in (3c) is replaced in (3d) by the complement clause *that he was still handsome.* The complement clauses can be analysed as occupying noun-phrase slots.

(3) a. Anne astonished her father.
     b. That Captain Wentworth married Anne astonished her father.
     c. Sir Walter Elliott imagined the scene.
     d. Sir Walter Elliott imagined that he was still handsome.

Time adverbs such as *yesterday* occur at the beginning of a clause or at the end of the verb phrase, as in (4), and adverbial clauses of time typically occur in the same positions, as in (5).

(4) a. Yesterday Lydia eloped with Wickham.
     b. Lydia eloped with Wickham yesterday.
(5) a. When Lydia went to Brighton, she eloped with Wickham.
     b. Lydia eloped with Wickham when she went to Brighton.

Adverbial clauses of reason behave in a similar fashion. Compare (6) with the phrase *because of the strike* and (7) with the clause *because the bus drivers were on strike.* Both can precede or follow the main clause, and both are optional (adjuncts).

(6) a. Because of the strike the commuters travelled by army lorry.
     b. The commuters travelled by army lorry because of the strike.
(7) a. Because the bus drivers were on strike, the commuters travelled by army lorry.
     b. The commuters travelled by army lorry because the bus drivers were on strike.

Clauses of concession and condition can also be seen as parallel to phrases. Example (8c) in Chapter 6, reproduced here as (8), can be rephrased as (9).

(8) Although Mr D'Arcy disliked Mrs Bennet he married Elizabeth.
(9) In spite of his dislike of Mrs Bennet, Mr D'Arcy married Elizabeth.

The phrase *in spite of* is not obviously a concession phrase, whereas *yesterday* and *because of the strike* are clearly time and reason phrases respectively. Example (9) nonetheless expresses a concession.

Example (8e) in Chapter 6 is repeated below as (10). It can be rephrased and split into two sentences, as in (11).

(10) If Emma had left Hartfield, Mr Woodhouse would have been unhappy.

(11)   Emma might have left Hartfield. In that case Mr Woodhouse would have been very unhappy.

Another possible rephrasing is *With Emma away from Hartfield, Mr Woodhouse will be very unhappy*, but there is controversy, to be discussed later, as to whether sequences such as *With Emma away from Hartfield* should be analysed as a phrase or as a kind of clause. In any case, the essential point is that most kinds of adverbial clause can be seen as substituting for adverbial phrases; we can state precisely where the phrases occur in a clause, and we can specify where the adverbial clauses occur, though rather less precisely.

Let us review where the discussion has brought us. Traditional definitions of sentence talk of a grammatical unit built up from smaller units. The smaller units (phrases and clauses) are linked to each other by various head–modifier relations (marked by the sorts of devices discussed in Chapter 9); a given phrase or clause can only occur in certain slots inside sentences. Sentences themselves cannot be described as occurring in any particular slot in a piece of text. This definition implies that the sentence has a certain sort of unity, being grammatically complete, and has a degree of semantic independence which enables it to stand on its own independent of context. We have seen that the above definition applies better to main clauses. Sentences are better treated as units of discourse into which writers group clauses. Without going into detail, we should note that clauses are recognisable in all types of spoken and written language but that no reliable criteria exist for the recognition of sentences in spontaneous speech. Subordinate clauses are indeed grammatically complete in themselves and their patterns of occurrence can be specified, but they cannot stand on their own independent of context.

We have worked our way towards the following position. We can describe where words occur in phrases, where phrases occur in clauses and where clauses occur in sentences. We can describe how words combine to form phrases, phrases to form clauses, and clauses to form sentences. In contrast, we cannot describe where sentences occur, and describing how sentences combine to make up a discourse or text is very different from analysing the structure of phrases and clauses. Finally, there are dense bundles of dependencies among the constituents of clauses; there is the occasional dependency relation across clause boundaries but none across sentence boundaries (in English). Links across sentence boundaries are better treated as binders tying small units together into a large piece of coherent text.

All the above are reasons for recognising the clause as a unit between phrase and sentence.

7.3 More properties of subordinate clauses

We turn now to other similarities and differences between main and subordinate clauses. The subordinate clauses in a given sentence are to a large extent grammatically independent of the main clause. They cannot stand on their own (in writing, at any rate), but the main clause does not control the choice of verb and other constituents, nor the choice of participant roles, tense, aspect and modal verbs. (The choices must make semantic sense, but that is a different question.) Compare the variants of the complement clause in (12).

(12) a. We heard that Captain Benwick would marry Louisa Hayter/ that Mary Hayter was a hypochondriac/that Admiral Croft was always accompanied by his wife.
b. We hear that Captain Benwick has married Louisa Hayter/that Captain Benwick married Louisa Hayter/that Captain Benwick is marrying/that Captain Benwick will marry Louisa Hayter.
c. We heard that Captain Benwick might marry/must have married Louisa Hayter.

In (12a), two of the complement clauses are active and the last one is passive. One complement clause is a copula construction, *that Mary Hayter was a hypochondriac*, while the other two are not. In (12b), one complement clause has a Perfect verb – *has married*, the second has a simple past tense – *married*, the third has a present-tense verb – *is marrying*, and the fourth has a future-tense verb – *will marry*. (See Chapter 13 for a discussion of tense.) In (12c), the complement clauses have different modal verbs, *might marry* vs *must (have) married*.

Subordinate clauses are, however, subject to a number of constraints that do not apply to main clauses. For instance, main clauses can be declarative, interrogative or imperative, as shown in (13a–c). (See the discussion of these terms in Chapter 3.)

(13) a. Captain Wentworth wrote a letter to Anne Elliott.
[DECLARATIVE]
b. Did Captain Wentworth write a letter to Anne Elliott?
[INTERROGATIVE]
c. Write a letter to Anne Elliott. [IMPERATIVE]

Subordinate clauses are not free with respect to choice of declarative, interrogative and imperative syntax. For example, relative clauses, adverbial clauses and most types of complement clause must have declarative syntax, as shown in (14).

(14) a. *Because did Marianne love Willoughby, she refused to

believe that he had deserted her. [Because Marianne loved Willoughby ...]

b. *If did Emma leave Hartfield, Mr Woodhouse would be unhappy. [If Emma left Hartfield ...]

c. *When did Fanny return, she found Tom Bertram very ill. [When Fanny returned ...]

d. *The cottage which did Mrs Dashwood accept was rather small. [... which Mrs Dashwood accepted ...]

e. *Catherine feared that was the Abbey haunted. [Catherine feared that the Abbey was haunted]

The phrase 'most types of complement clause' was used because a number of verbs allow a type of complement that is traditionally called 'indirect question'. Examples are given in (15).

(15) a. Elizabeth asked whether/if Mr Bingley would return to Netherfield.

b. The girls wondered who Mr Bennet had received in his library.

The clauses introduced by *whether/if* and *who* are indirect questions. Example (15a) is completely declarative in syntax, apart from the WH word *whether*; (15b) is partly declarative and partly interrogative – declarative in the order of noun phrase and auxiliary verb (*Mr Bennet had received*) but interrogative in having the WH word *who* at the front of the clause. These subordinate clauses can be seen as corresponding to the main interrogative clauses *Will Mr Bingley return to Netherfield?* and *Who did Mr Bennet receive in his library?*

Interestingly, contemporary spoken English has the type of complement clause in (16). It is normal for spoken English in all sorts of formal and informal contexts and is beginning to turn up in written texts.

(16) a. She asked was Alison coming to the party.

b. We were wondering who did you meet at the conference.

The complement clauses have straightforward interrogative syntax – *was Alison coming to the party* and *who did you meet at the conference*. These examples could be uttered with pauses between the clauses and with each clause having its own intonation pattern, but typically there is no pause and the whole utterance has one single intonation pattern. Note that although the complement clauses in (16) have interrogative syntax, they do not invalidate the statement that subordinate clauses are typically limited to declarative syntax.

Subordinate clauses are limited in other respects. Main clauses, but not subordinate clauses, are open to a wide range of syntactic constructions. Consider the examples in (17).

(17) **Prepositional phrase fronting**
   a. In came Aunt Norris. [cf. Aunt Norris came in]/Into the room came Aunt Norris.
   b. She said that in came Aunt Norris./She said that into the room came Aunt Norris.
   c. *The person who in came at that moment was Aunt Norris./ *The person who into the room came at that moment was Aunt Norris.
   d. *Because in came Aunt Norris, Fanny stopped talking./*Because into the room came Aunt Norris, Fanny stopped talking.
   e. *When in came Aunt Norris, Fanny stopped talking./*When into the room came Aunt Norris, Fanny stopped talking.

The construction has a preposition in first position followed by the main verb followed by the subject NP. It can occur in declarative main clauses, and in complement clauses – compare (17b) – but not in relative clauses or adverbial clauses.

(18) **Negative fronting**
   a. Never had Sir Thomas been so offended. (Sir Thomas had never been so offended.)
   b. They realised that never had Sir Thomas been so offended.
   c. *The person who never had he been so offended was Sir Thomas.
   d. *Because never had Sir Thomas been so offended, even Mr Yates left.
   e. *When never had Sir Thomas been so offended, Mr Yates left.

Example (18b) can be derived from *Sir Thomas had never been so offended*. *Never* moves to the front of the clause and *Sir Thomas* and *had* change places. As with preposition fronting, the construction is acceptable in main clauses and complement clauses but not in relative or adverbial clauses.

(19) **Tag questions**
   a. Dr Grantly habitually ate too much rich food, didn't he?
   b. *We realised that Dr Grantly died because he ate too much rich food, didn't he?
   c. *The person who ate too much rich food didn't he was Dr Grantly.
   d. *Because Dr Grantly ate too much rich food didn't he, he died of apoplexy.
   e. *When Dr Grantly died of apoplexy didn't he, Mary Crawford went to live with his wife.

Didn't he? in (19a) is a **tag question**, so named because the structure consists of a declarative clause, *Dr Grantly habitually ate too much rich food*, with a question tagged on at the end, *didn't he?* Tag questions consist of verbs such as *did, might, can* and so on plus a pronoun, and possibly with the negation marker *-n't* or *not*.

Tag questions do not occur in any subordinate clause. Note that in an example such as *Edmund knew that Dr Grantly died of apoplexy, didn't he?*, the tag question relates to the verb in the main clause, *knew*, and not to *died of apoplexy*. Note also that the examples in (19) are intended to be taken as written language and that spoken utterances must be supposed to carry a single intonation pattern and to have no breaks. The latter stipulation is necessary, because speakers do produce utterances such as *because Dr Grantly ate too much rich food*, break off the utterance and ask the tag question, and then, having received an answer, go back to the main clause. That type of interrupted syntax is not relevant for present purposes.

The data in (14)–(19) suggest that there is a hierarchy of subordination. Complement clauses are the least subordinate and allow preposition fronting, negative fronting and, depending on the head verb, interrogative structures. Relative clauses and adverbial clauses are most subordinate. They exclude all the constructions in (14)–(19), together with interrogative and imperative structures.

The position of some adverbial clauses on the hierarchy is not straightforward but is affected by their position in sentences. As (7) shows, adverbial clauses of reason can precede or follow the main clause. When they follow the main clause, they allow negative fronting and preposition fronting, but not when they precede it. This suggests that in the latter position they are more subordinate. Consider the examples in (20), and note the examples in (21) and (22) which show that adverbial clauses of time and concession do not behave this way.

(20) a. Fanny stopped talking because in came Aunt Norris.
     b. *Because in came Aunt Norris Fanny stopped talking.
     c. Mr Yates left because never had Sir Thomas been so offended.
     d. *Because never had Sir Thomas been so offended, Mr Yates left.

(21) a. *Fanny stopped talking when in came Aunt Norris.
     b. *When in came Aunt Norris Fanny stopped talking.

(22) a. *Fanny continued talking although in came Aunt Norris.
     b. *Although in came Aunt Norris, Fanny continued talking.

Adverbial clauses of reason following the main clause seem to play a different role from the one they play preceding the main clause. It has

been suggested that adverbial clauses preceding the main clause serve as signposts to the text, whereas adverbial clauses following the main clause serve as comments on what has been said or written. In conversation, adverbial clauses may (emphasis on *may*) be separated from the main clause by a pause and may have their own intonation pattern, though clearly these considerations are irrelevant to written text.

It has been proposed that sequences of main clause + adverbial clause of reason come close to being conjoined clauses, that is, clauses of equal status. This proposal seems on the right lines, and it opens an interesting view of *when* clauses that have been (mistakenly) regarded as subordinate. Compare (21a), reproduced as (23a), and (23b).

(23) a. *Fanny stopped talking when in came Aunt Norris.
      b. Fanny had just stopped talking when in came Aunt Norris.

Example (23a) presents two events as simultaneous: Fanny stopped talking and Aunt Norris came in. Example (23b) presents one event as following the other: Fanny stopped talking, after which Aunt Norris came in. It is not entirely clear why (23b) is acceptable, but it is worth pointing out that *when* can be replaced by *and then*, that is, by an expression that overtly conjoins the two clauses and fits with the notion of main clause + adverbial clause as two conjoined clauses. Example (23a) does not allow the substitution, since the two events are presented as simultaneous

7.4 Finite and non-finite clauses

The clauses examined in this chapter all have a finite verb. Much contemporary analysis recognises a category of **non-finite clauses** – sequences of words which lack a finite verb but nonetheless are treated as subordinate clauses. Examples are given in (24), with the non-finite clauses in italics.

(24) a. Fanny regretted *talking to Mary.*
      b. Henry wanted *to marry Fanny.*
      c. *Mrs Bennet having taken the others upstairs,* Mr Bingley proposed to Jane.
      d. All Mr Collins does is *praise Lady de Bourg.*
      e. Lady de Bourg tried *to persuade Elizabeth to renounce Mr D'Arcy.*

Such sequences were until recently treated as phrases – for instance, *to marry Fanny* in (24b) was described as an **infinitive** phrase, and *talking to Mary* in (24a) as a **gerund** phrase. There are, however, good reasons for treating them as clauses. Like the classical finite subordinate clauses, they contain a verb and a full set of modifiers – *marry* in (24b) has *Fanny* as a complement, *talking* in (24a) has *to Mary* as a directional complement, and *having taken* in (24c) has *Mrs Bennet* and *the others* as complements and *upstairs* as a directional complement. They can have aspect, as shown by (25a, c) which are Perfect and by (25b) which is progressive.

(25) a. Henry wanted *to have married Fanny before Edmund returned.*
      b. *Mrs Bennet taking the others upstairs*, Mr Bingley gave a sigh of relief
      c. Fanny regretted *having talked to Mary.*
      d. What Mr Collins is doing is *praising Lady de Bourg.*

Against the above data must be set the fact that non-finite constructions are highly limited in their grammar. Examples (24a–e) exclude tense and modal verbs such as CAN, MAY, MUST. They exclude interrogative and imperative constructions and do not allow prepositional phrase fronting or negative fronting. In spite of (25), BE is excluded from (24a) and (25b) – see (26a, b). HAVE is excluded from (24d) – see (26c).

(26) a. *Fanny regretted *being talking to Mary.*
      b. *Mrs Bennet being taking the others upstairs*, Mr Bingley gave a sigh of relief.
      c. *All Mr Collins has done is *have praised Lady de Bourg.*

The non-finite constructions do allow some modality to be signalled, that is, events can be presented as necessary, or requiring permission, or requiring ability, as in (27a–c).

(27) a. Fanny regretted *having to talk to Aunt Norris.*   [necessity]
      b. Julia and Maria wanted *to be allowed to perform a play.*   [permission]
      c. Edmund wanted Fanny *to be able to ride a horse.*   [ability]

The presentation of an event as possible is excluded, or at least very rare.

(28) *Henry wanted *to possibly marry Fanny.*

As shown by (12) above, in a given sentence, finite subordinate clauses have their own set of participants independent of the participants in the main clause. This is not true of most non-finite constructions. Consider (29), which brings us to the traditional concept of the **understood subject.**

(29) Henry wanted *to marry Fanny.*

The infinitive construction *to marry Fanny* has no overt subject noun phrase, but *Henry* is traditionally called the understood subject of *marry.* That is, traditionally it was recognised that (29) refers to two situations – Henry's wanting something, and someone's marrying Fanny. Furthermore, it was recognised that Henry is the person doing the wanting, so to speak, and also the person (in Henry's mind) marrying Fanny. The syntax is rather condensed relative to the semantic interpretation, since there is only one finite clause but two propositions, one for each situation. In contemporary terms, the notion of understood subject is translated into that of control. The subject of WANT is said to control the subject of the verb in the dependent infinitive. That is, there is a dependency relation between the infinitive and the subject of *wanted.* (See the discussion of 'subject' in Chapter 8.) Remember that in Chapter 1 the heads of phrases were described as controlling their modifiers, in the sense of determining how many modifiers could occur and what type. In connection with *Henry wanted to marry Fanny,* the noun phrase *Henry* determines the interpretation of another, invisible, noun phrase, the subject of *marry.* The technical term for this relationship is 'control'; it is important to note that 'control' has these different uses.

In (30), a similar analysis is applied to the gerund, the *-ing* phrase that complements *loved,* where the understood subject of *talking* is *Fanny.* In contemporary terms, the subject of LOVE is held to control the subject of the dependent gerund – here, the subject of *loved* controls the subject of *talking to Mary.*

(30)   Fanny loved talking to Mary.

With respect to (31), traditional analysis recognises one clause but more than one potential situation: Lady de Bourg tried to do something, Lady de Bourg persuade Elizabeth, and Elizabeth renounce Mr D'Arcy. The subject of *tried* controls the *subject* of the dependent infinitive, here *to persuade. To persuade* in turn has a dependent infinitive – *to renounce.* The object of persuade, *Elizabeth,* controls the subject of *to renounce.*

(31)   Lady de Bourg tried to persuade Elizabeth to renounce Mr D'Arcy.

What the above facts boil down to is that on the hierarchy of clauseness, main clauses outrank everything else, and subordinate finite clauses outrank by a good head the candidate non-finite subordinate clauses. Why then do contemporary analysts see the non-finite sequences in (24) as clauses, albeit non-finite? The answer is that they give priority to the fact that non-finite and finite sequences have the same set of complements and adjuncts. Verbs exercise the same control over the types and number of their complements in finite and non-finite constructions; for example, PUT requires to its right a noun phrase and a directional phrase, in both *The child put the toy on the table* and *The child tried to put the toy on the table*. Example (24c) has an overt subject, *Mrs Bennet*, and the other non-finite constructions have understood subjects.

The latter ties in with the important business of semantic interpretation. Finite clauses are held to express propositions, and so are non-finite clauses, once the understood subject is, so to speak, filled in. (Note that prioritising data, facts, tasks and various theoretical concerns is an integral part of any analytic work. Raw data are dumb until they are interpreted in the light of this or that theory and put to work in a solution to this or that theoretical problem.)

What are called **free participles**, adjuncts containing *-ing* forms, pose interesting problems. Consider (32a, b), which are the same construction as exemplified by (24c).

(32) a. Knowing the country well, he took a short cut.
      b. Slamming the door, he ran down the steps.

The problem is this. The non-finite constructions in (24) can be straightforwardly correlated with finite clauses, *Henry marries Fanny, Fanny talks to Mary, Mrs Bennet had taken the others upstairs* and so on. Example (32a) contains *knowing*, but in spite of this being called a free participle, KNOW does not have *-ing* forms that combine with BE, as shown by (33).

(33) *He was knowing the country well.

Slamming the door in (32b) is equally problematic. The free participle sequence cannot be related to *When/while he was slamming the door* but only to *When he had slammed the door*. That is, the path from the free participle to the time clause would involve the introduction of a different auxiliary, HAVE. In general, free participles are best treated as a non-finite type of clause with only a very indirect connection, whatever it might be, with finite clauses.

Non-finite constructions with infinitives and participles at least contain a verb form, even if it is non-finite. Some analysts even propose treating the parts in bold in (34) as clauses, although they have no verb form of any kind.

(34) a. *When ripe*, these apples will be delicious.
      b. He left the train *with somebody else's wallet in his pocket*.
      c. She walked up the hill, *her rucksack on her back*.
      d   We found the cage *empty*.

Example (34a) comes closest to a clause, in that the candidate sequence contains *when*, which looks like a complementiser. Example (34a) could be seen as resulting from ellipsis, the ellipted constituents being a noun phrase and some form of BE: *when they are ripe* —> *when ripe*. Examples

(34b, c) are unlikely candidates, on the grounds that they cannot be easily correlated with a main clause. It is impossible to insert an -*ing* form into (34b) *He left the train with somebody else's wallet being in his pocket*: in fact, this construction is used only preceding a main clause and typically in order to present one situation as the cause of another; compare the earlier example *With Emma having left Hartfield Mr Woodhouse was unhappy*, and *With somebody else's wallet being in his pocket, he was glad not to be stopped by any policemen.*

None of the above contradicts the semantic facts that, for example, (34c) and (34d) express several propositions: 'She walked up the hill' + 'She had her rucksack' + 'Her rucksack was on her back' for (34c) and 'We found the cage' + 'The cage was empty' for (34d). The moral is that while semantic facts should be taken into account, an analysis of syntax should never depend on semantic facts alone. The structures in (34) express propositions but are not even non-finite clauses.

Summary

The traditional distinction between clause and sentence is important. A main clause combines with one or more subordinate clauses to form a sentence. Where different clauses occur in sentences can be described, as can where phrases occur inside clauses. Where sentences occur in texts cannot be described except very loosely. Sentences can be regarded as a low-level unit of discourse. Main clauses allow a very wide range of syntactic constructions and all the distinctions of aspect, tense and mood. In contrast, subordinate clauses allow a smaller range of syntactic constructions and fewer distinctions of aspect, tense and mood. There is a hierarchy of subordinate clauses. Complement clauses are least subordinate, relative and adverbial clauses are most subordinate. What were traditionally regarded as infinitive and gerund phrases are now treated as clauses on the ground that they express propositions and, like finite clauses, consist of a verb plus complements and adjuncts.

Exercises

1. Pick out the non-finite clauses in the following examples. Say whether each non-finite clause is an infinitive, a gerund or a free participle and what the understood subject is.

   1. She tried to learn two languages simultaneously to a high level inside three months.
   2. I hate travelling to Glasgow by the M8 at this time of year.

3. Having looked at all the exercises very carefully, we concluded that the marking had been too lenient.
4. Sheila quickly hiding something under the chair when I came in, I assumed that she had been buying my Christmas present.
5. I don't understand Imogen's being so keen to spend her holidays tramping tirelessly round art galleries.
6. With all the children coming home for Christmas and the New Year, I'm going to take the dogs for long walks.
7. His car sold, he set off on foot for Tighnabruaich.

2. Indirect questions

English has two types of interrogative constructions: direct questions and indirect questions. Direct questions are, as the name suggests, put directly: for example, *When did you phone?*, *Did you remember to buy potatoes?*, *How long is this essay?*, *Who paid for the meal?* In indirect questions, interrogative structures such as the above are the complement of verbs such as ASK, WONDER, DEMAND and so on. Some of the examples below are taken from grammars of English, while other examples are taken from various types of spontaneously produced English (*spontaneously* in the sense that they were not thought up for the purposes of tutorial material but were used by speakers of English in the ordinary course of speaking or writing.)

1. Describe the syntax of the indirect questions – that is, specify the type of question (WH or yes–no) and whether the word order is direct or indirect.
2. Try to decide which indirect question constructions
   (a) you have heard used in speech or seen in writing;
   (b) you would accept in a piece of written work (say, from a someone learning English as a second language);
   (c) you would use in formal writing (say, an essay or a job application).

1. I wondered when the plane would leave.
2. They were trying to decide where the best place was to go on holiday.
3. We still have the problem of how we are to fund the extra resources.
4. John asked me whether I was ready yet.
5. Mary told him how brave he was.
6. I can't remember now what was the reason for it.
7. If they got a carpet, they had to decide where was the best place to put it.

8. No one is sure how long are the passages leading off from this centre.

9. But the thought did cross my mind as to what is the rate of burglary per hour in Edinburgh.

10. The question arises as to what language should they be literate in.

11. The problem still remains of what is the resource-holding body.

12. You were shouting at me about why had I not done something.

13. We would like them to share what are their forecasts.

14. The real issue is whether this institution is governed dictatorially from the top or do we have a democratic college.

15. In the diagram on the next page I have tried to represent my own personal opinion about whether these verbs can take a human subject and if so do they necessarily require an object which is either water or another liquid.

8 Grammatical functions

8.1 Introduction

We have seen that in a given clause the verb can be regarded as the head, controlling the other major phrases. Two sets of concepts bear on the relationship between the verb in a clause and its complements; one is the set of grammatical functions or grammatical relations, that is, subject, direct object, indirect object/second object and oblique object, and the other is the set of roles such as Agent and Patient. The first three terms used to be familiar to anyone who studied any of the foreign languages normally offered in British schools – French, German, Spanish, Latin, Russian. They are in constant use in grammars of languages from every part of the world and have been deployed for centuries in the study of European languages, yet it turns out to be far from straightforward to define the concepts, and it has yet to be determined whether they apply to languages which differ greatly from English in their grammar.

8.2 Subject

The most complex grammatical function is that of subject. Consider the example in (1).

(1) The tigers hunt prey at night.

Tigers precedes the verb. It agrees with the verb in number, as becomes clear when it is made singular: *The tiger hunts its prey at night.* In the active construction, it is never marked by any preposition. The corresponding full passive clause (see Chapter 3 on constructions) is *Prey is hunted by the tigers at night*; in the passive clause, the subject of (1), *the tigers*, turns up inside the prepositional phrase *by the tigers*.

The above criteria – agreement in number with the verb, never being preceded by a preposition, occurring in the *by* phrase in the passive – are grammatical, and the noun they pick out in a given clause is the **grammatical subject** of that clause. *Tigers* has another interesting property:

it refers to the Agent in the situation described by (1). Many analysts consider that *tigers* refers to the Agent in the passive sentence too, although it is inside the *by* prepositional phrase and at the end of the sentence. They call *tigers* the **logical subject**, by which is meant that in either syntactic construction *tigers* denotes the Agent. That is, its role in the situation does not change.

Other analysts maintain that in the passive sentence *tigers* no longer denotes the Agent but rather the Path by which the action reaches and affects the prey. Such arguments lead us into a very old and unresolved controversy as to whether language corresponds directly to objective reality or whether it reflects a mental representation of the outside world. For the moment, we put this controversy aside; but it will return (possibly to haunt us) when we take up the topic of roles. All we need do here is note the assumptions that lie behind the notion of logical subject, and to understand that in any case the grammatical subject NP in an active construction of English typically denotes an Agent. This follows from the fact that most verbs in English denote actions.

A third type of subject is the **psychological subject**. In (1), *tigers* is the starting point of the message; it denotes the entities about which the speaker wishes to say something, as the traditional formula puts it. Example (1) is a neutral sentence: it has a neutral word order, and the three types of subject coincide on the NP *tigers*. Psychological subject and grammatical subject need not coincide. In *This prey tigers hunted*, the psychological subject is *this prey*. (It is what was called 'topic' in (7d) in Chapter 3 on constructions.)

In contemporary linguistic analysis, the notion of psychological subject has long been abandoned, since it encompasses various concepts that can only be treated properly if they are teased apart. Again, the details need not concern us. What is important is that in sentences such as (1) the grammatical subject noun phrase typically denotes the Agent and typically denotes the entity which speakers announce and of which they then make a predication.

It is the regular coincidence of grammatical subject, Agent and psychological subject in English and other languages of Europe that makes the notion of subject so natural to native speakers and to analysts. Here, we take the grammatical criteria to be the most important and explore them further. Consider the examples in (2).

(2) a. Fiona hoped to meet the Prime Minister.
   b. Susan intends to reach Kashgar.
   c. Arthur tried to bake a cake.

All these examples contain infinitive phrases: *to meet the PM*, *to reach*

Kashgar, to bake a cake. As was discussed in Chapter 7, such infinitives are nowadays regarded as non-finite clauses, one of their properties being that they have understood subjects: for example, *Fiona* is the understood subject of *meet the PM*; Fiona is, so to speak, doing the hoping and Fiona is the person who is to do the meeting, and similarly for *Susan* in (2b) and *Arthur* in (2c).

The infinitive *meet* in (2a) is dependent on the main verb *hoped*, and the grammatical subject of the main verb, *Fiona*, is said to control the understood subject of the infinitive.

In the sentences in (2), the main verbs have only one complement, the infinitive. In the examples in (3), the verbs have two complements, a noun phrase and an infinitive.

(3) a. Fiona persuaded Arthur to bake a cake.
    b. Susan wanted Jane to study German.

In (3a, b), the verbs *persuaded* and *wanted* are followed by a noun phrase, *Arthur* and *Jane*, and then by an infinitive phrase. These infinitive phrases too have understood subjects controlled by the noun phrases *Arthur* and *Jane* to the right of the verb; Arthur underwent the persuasion and did the baking; Jane was the target of Susan's wishes and was to do the studying. Suppose we expand (3a) to include the 'missing' constituents:

(3a') Fiona persuaded Arthur: Arthur to bake a cake.

Suppose we relate the infinitive to a finite clause: *Arthur baked a cake*. The path from the finite clause to the infinitive involves deleting a constituent; the affected constituent is always the grammatical subject of the non-finite clause, which is why analysts see the subject as pivotal to the infinitive construction.

The sentences in (4) exemplify a different construction.

(4) a. Ayala went to the ball. Ayala chatted to Jonathan Stubbs.
    b. Ayala went to the ball and chatted to Jonathan Stubbs.

The two sentences in (4a) yield the single sentence in (4b) by the ellipsis of the grammatical subject, *Ayala*, in the second sentence. Only the grammatical subject can be ellipted. Example (5a) cannot be converted into (5b) by the ellipsis of the non-subject *Ayala* in the second sentence.

(5) a. Ayala went to the ball. Jonathan Stubbs chatted to Ayala.
    b. *Ayala went to the ball and Jonathan Stubbs chatted to.

It does not matter whether the grammatical subject NP denotes an Agent, as is demonstrated by the combining of active and passive sentences in (6).

(6) a. Ayala went to the ball. Ayala was chatted to by Jonathan Stubbs.
     b. Ayala went to the ball and was chatted to by Jonathan Stubbs.

In this construction, too, the grammatical subject is pivotal, in the sense that it is a grammatical subject that is omitted on the way from the (a) to the (b) examples. Furthermore, the understood subject of the second clause in (4b) and (6b) is controlled by the initial grammatical subject.

A third construction in which the grammatical subject NP is central is exemplified in (7).

(7) a. All the Tringles came to Merle Park.
     b. The Tringles all came to Merle Park.
     c. Both Jane and Elizabeth were at home.
     d. Jane and Elizabeth were both at home.

In (7b), the word *all* is part of the noun phrase *all the Tringles*. That noun phrase is the subject, and *all* can 'float' out of the NP to a position next the finite verb, as in (7b). Similarly, *both* can be part of the subject noun phrase as in (7c) but can float to the same position, as in (7d).

Only subject NPs allow *all* and *both* to float. In (8a), *all* is part of the non-subject phrase *all the foxes* and cannot float to the left of the finite verb, as shown by the unacceptable (8b), nor to the right, as in the unacceptable (8c). Nor can *both* in (8c) and (8d).

(8) a. Larry Twentyman hunted all the foxes.
     b. *Larry Twentyman all hunted the foxes.
     c. *Larry Twentyman hunted the foxes all.
     d. George built both the houses.
     e. *George both built the houses.
     f. *George built the houses both.

As with the missing subject in the conjoined clauses in (5) and (6), quantifiers can float out of subject noun phrases in both active and passive clauses, as shown by (9a, b).

(9) a. All the foxes were hunted by Larry Twentyman.
     b The foxes were all hunted by Larry Twentyman.

One final property of grammatical subjects is worth mentioning, namely that just as subjects control the understood subjects of non-finite clauses, so they control the interpretation of reflexive pronouns inside single clauses. This is shown in (10), where *Augusta* and *herself* refer to the same woman called Augusta.

(10) Augusta blamed herself for what happened.

In the above discussion, we have talked of grammatical subject noun phrases as having particular properties, but to talk in this way is to take the notion of grammatical subject for granted. We present the state of affairs more accurately if we say that in English various properties attach to noun phrases: denoting an Agent, specifying the entity the speaker wishes to say something about, acting as the pivot of various constructions (coordination, infinitives, *both* and *all* floating, reflexives), being involved in person and number agreement with the finite verb. In the neutral active declarative construction of English, these properties converge on one NP, which is accorded the title of grammatical subject.

As the discussion of psychological subject showed, the properties do not always converge on one noun phrase. The psychological subject of (11) is *these documents*, which does not agree with *is* in number and person and is not the grammatical subject.

(11)   These documents Elizabeth is checking at this very moment.

One property must be added to the list. It is not relevant to English (apart from the pronoun system) but it is central to other Indo-European languages such as Russian. The property is that of taking nominative case, as exemplified in (12).

(12)   a.   Ivan tolknul Mashu ('Ivan – pushed – Masha')
       b.   Masha tolknula Ivana ('Masha – pushed – Ivan')

In (12a), *Ivan* is in the nominative case (as the traditional formula puts it) and *Mashu* is in the accusative case. In (12b), *Masha* is in the nominative case and *Ivana* is in the accusative case. Analogous changes only show up in the pronouns in English, as in *I pushed him* and *He pushed me*.

We conclude this discussion of subject by listing the relevant properties and by pointing out that the list employs concepts that were important for the discussion of constructions in Chapter 3 and of word classes in Chapter 4. In our examination of constructions, in particular the idea of constructions forming a system, we appealed to the concept of a basic construction, which was [DECLARATIVE, ACTIVE, POSITIVE]. This basic construction allows the greatest range of tense, aspect, mood and voice (see Chapters 12 and 13 on grammar and semantics); instances of this construction are the easiest to turn into relative or interrogative clauses; they take the greatest range of adverbs. They are semantically more basic than other clauses; in order to understand, for example, *Kate wasn't helping* and *Was Kate helping?*, it is necessary to understand *Kate was helping.*

The list of properties that we are to establish relates to the basic construction. In the discussion of word classes, we distinguished between syntactic and morpho-syntactic properties. Subjects have the following major properties:

Syntactic properties:
- control of **reflexives**, as in (10)
- control of *all* and *both* floating, as in (7) and (9)
- functioning as pivot in infinitives and coordinate constructions, as in (3), (4) and (6).

Morpho-syntactic properties:
- being involved in person and number links with the finite verb
- being in the nominative case.

There are two semantic properties. One is simply that grammatical subjects typically refer to Agents. The second is that they refer to entities that exist independently of the action or state denoted by the main verb, whereas there are many verbs whose direct object does not have this property (see section 8.3 below on direct objects.) For example, in *Skilled masons built the central tower in less than a year* the direct object, *the central tower*, denotes an entity that does not exist independently of the action for the simple reason that it is created by the activity of building. Note that the passive clause *The central tower was built by skilled masons in less than a year* does not contradict what has just been said. *The central tower* is certainly a subject and denotes the entity created by the building activity, but the passive construction is not basic.

8.3 Direct object

The concept of direct object is as widely used as that of subject and has just as long a tradition. Nonetheless, it too turns out to be elusive. As with grammatical subject, it is possible to provide criteria for direct objects in English, but the criteria do not necessarily carry over to other languages. Keeping to the [ACTIVE DECLARATIVE] construction, we can say that in sentences such as (13) the NP following the verb is the direct object.

(13) a. Louise broke the cup.
      b. Alison drove the car.
      c. Martha chewed the bread.

We can say that the direct object NP is never preceded by a preposition – in the sentence *Martha chewed on the bread, bread* is not a direct object, and the entity it denotes is not completely affected by the action of chewing – compare the discussion of Patients in Chapter 11. Neutral active declarative sentences typically have passive counterparts. One of the properties of the English NPs called direct objects is that they correspond to the grammatical subjects of passive sentences. This is shown in (14a–c), the passive counterparts of (13a–c).

(14)   a. The cup was broken by Louise.
       b. The car was driven by Alison.
       c. The bread was chewed by Martha.

We can say that direct object NPs typically refer to Patients.

Even for English alone, difficulties appear. One problem is that the criteria, even with the help of the weasel adverb *typically*, do not extend unequivocally to other constructions. Consider the passive sentences in (15).

(15)   a. How is a girl to be chatted to if she does not go out? (Anthony Trollope, *Ayala*).
       b. These fields were marched over by all the armies of Europe.

These passive sentences contain grammatical subjects (on the criteria applicable to English), but their active counterparts do not contain direct objects – compare (16).

(16)   a. How is someone to chat to a girl if she does not go out?
       b. All the armies of Europe marched over these fields.

In (16), the correspondents of the grammatical subjects in (15) are inside prepositional phrases: *to a girl, over these fields*. The examples show that either more than direct objects can be converted to grammatical subjects in the passive construction or we have to regard *chat to* and *march over* as single verbs that take direct objects.

Another difficulty with English is that some apparent active transitive clauses have no corresponding passive: *That car weighs two tons* is not matched by **Two tons are weighed by that car, Arthur measures six feet* is not matched by **Six feet are measured by Arthur, Her daughters resemble Lucy* is not matched by **Lucy is resembled by her daughters* and *The cage contained a panda* cannot be converted to **A panda was contained by the cage*. It has been suggested that, for example, in *The cage contained a panda*, the panda is not a Patient (compare Chapter 11), but nobody has suggested that *the panda* is not a direct object.

In spite of the reservations mentioned above, in the [NEUTRAL, ACTIVE DECLARATIVE] construction of English we do have criteria for recognising direct objects with most verbs combining with two NPs. (We exclude the copula construction, 'copula' including BE, GET, SEEM,

BECOME and others.) Another criterion that has been proposed for direct objects in English relates to the positions occupied by particles such as *back*. Where a verb combines with two NPs, the particle occurs after the verb, but before or after the direct object NP, as in (17).

(17) a. Ayala sent back the diamond necklace.
      b. Ayala sent the diamond necklace back.

In clauses with three NPs, the occurrence of the particle is limited.

(18) a. Ayala sent her cousin the diamond necklace.
      b. *Ayala sent back her cousin the diamond necklace.
      c. ?Ayala sent her cousin back the diamond necklace.
      d. Ayala sent her cousin the diamond necklace back.

Example (18b) is bad, although *back* is in the same position as (17a), between the verb and the immediately following noun phrase. Example (18c) is not acceptable to all speakers, although *back* follows the NP immediately to the right of the verb. To be balanced against this criterion is the fact that *her cousin* in (18a) can become the grammatical subject of the corresponding passive: *Her cousin was sent back the diamond necklace by Ayala.* Which of the two criteria is to be given precedence: the position of *back* or becoming grammatical subject of the passive?

Another complication that deserves mention is that pronouns behave differently from full NPs with respect to *back*. Example (18c) merits no more than a question mark, but the substitution of *him* for *her cousin* yields an acceptable sentence: *Ayala sent him back the diamond necklace.* (Interestingly, other particles, such as *away*, exclude potential direct objects. They allow prepositional phrases, as in *Ayala sent away the diamond necklace to her cousin*; but compare *Ayala sent her cousin away the diamond necklace.*)

The general picture of direct object in English is fragmented, unlike the picture of grammatical subject. The latter can be recognised for any construction, but for direct object only one construction provides solid evidence, the basic active declarative construction, both in itself and in its relationship with the passive. As for the concept of subject, one criterion can be added for some languages other than English; as shown in (12a) and (12b), direct object nouns are in the accusative case.

8.4 Oblique object and indirect object

Recent work in syntax deploys the concept of oblique object; in English, any noun phrase that is the complement of a preposition is an oblique object, where the prepositional phrase is itself the complement of a verb. In (19), *to Onegin, to Egilsay* and *for Jane* are oblique objects.

(19) a. Tatiana wrote to Onegin.
      b. Magnus went to Egilsay.
      c. Frank bought a piano for Jane.

Phrases such as *to Onegin* used to be analysed as containing indirect object nouns, but this concept of indirect object is problematical. Grammars of English would merely refer to verbs such as TELL, SAY, SHOW and GIVE, which occur in the construction V NP₁ TO NP₂ or V NP₂ NP₁: compare *Celia gave the car to Ben* vs *Celia gave Ben the car*, where *the car* is NP₁ and *Ben* is NP₂. The indirect object was said to be the noun phrase preceded by *to*, and the relevant verbs were either listed individually or divided into classes labelled 'verbs of saying', 'verbs of giving' and so on in order to avoid the label 'indirect object' being assigned to phrases such as *to Dundee* in *He went to Dundee*.

In fact, it is difficult to separate indirect objects from adverbs of direction. It is sometimes suggested that the two can be distinguished on the grounds that indirect object NPs contain animate nouns, whereas adverbs of place contain inanimate nouns denoting countries, towns and other places. If this were correct, we would expect inanimate nouns not to occur immediately to the right of a verb such as *sent* in (20) and (21).

(20) a. Lucy sent a letter to Isadore.
      b. Lucy sent Isadore a letter.
(21) a. The Government sent an envoy to China.
      b. (*)The Government sent China an envoy.

It has been suggested that (21b) is not correct, but the fault is semantic and not syntactic. Example (21b) has the interpretation that a person is sent to China so that China can use him/her as an envoy. This is a rather unusual situation – at least out of context, (21b) seems odd. The oddness can be removed by substituting different lexical items, as in (22).

(22) The company sent China its senior mining engineers to help plan the new mines.

Example (22) presents China not just as a geographical area but as a body that is to benefit from the engineers. With the appropriate interpretation, then, an inanimate noun can occur to the right of the verb.

Another suggestion is that indirect objects can occur immediately to the right of the verb but not immediately to the right of genuine adverbs of direction. (Genuine adverbs of direction would not include *China* in (22).) This suggestion is correct, but it still fails to distinguish indirect *enjoyed all her other novels*) as opposed to an obligation placed on individuals by others or by circumstances (*I have to read that novel because there's an obligatory question on it in the exam*, or *I have to go to the dentist because the toothache keeps waking me up*). This analysis of *must* and *have to* does not fit the facts of usage. Speakers recognise *have got to* as expressing obligations placed on individuals by others or by circumstances. *Have to* is neutral, and *must* is peripheral for many speakers (as opposed to writers).

As mentioned in the paragraph following example (8) above, *have* and *have got to* are used for the expression of epistemic modality. The original meaning of *have* and *have got to* was and is deontic, that is, some action is necessary because circumstances make it so. The use of these verbs in examples such as *That has to be the worst joke I've ever heard* is more recent. Similarly, the use of *ought* and *should* has changed. Their original meaning is one of moral obligation, as in *He should help his friends, not laugh at them*. Another use, possibly derived from the moral-obligation interpretation, is exemplified in *The computer desk should hold together now that I've put in extra screws*. A moral obligation is weaker and more easily avoided than an obligation imposed by circumstances, and this difference between *ought* and *should* on the one hand and *have* and *have got to* on the other is reflected in the epistemic uses. Speakers who say *That book should be in the library* draw conclusions from whatever evidence is available to them, such as patterns of book-borrowing or the fact that they returned the book to the library just twenty minutes before. But they draw a much weaker conclusion than speakers who say *the book must be in the library*. The latter statement indicates that no other conclusion is possible, whereas *should* leaves room for the conclusion to be wrong.

Summary

The chapter title 'Grammar and semantics' reflects the central idea that certain distinctions in the grammars of languages (including the grammar of English) signal important distinctions of meaning. (Traditionally the label for the grammatical distinctions and associated meanings was 'grammatical categories'.) Case has to do with how languages signal the relationships between the verb and the nouns in a clause. In many languages, nouns consist of a central stem to which case endings (case suffixes) are added. Verb–noun relationships are also signalled by word order and prepositions, and the term 'case' has been extended to these devices. Gender has to do with the different classes of noun in a given language. In English, nouns divide into classes based largely on natural gender; that is, the gender class a noun belongs to is connected with whether the related pronoun is *he*, *she* or *it*. In other languages, nouns referring to inanimate objects fall into classes labelled 'masculine' or 'feminine', but the reasons have to do with the grammatical behaviour of the nouns and not their meaning. Mood has to do with the modes in which speakers and writers can present situations. They can make statements, ask questions or issue commands with respect to a situation. They can present a situation as a fact, as possible or as a necessary consequence of certain circumstances. They can present a situation as real, that is, as close to or actually happening in this world, or as unreal or irreal, as not happening in this world and even as so remote from this world that it will never happen.

Exercises

The following sentences contain modal verbs. Which of the verbs have epistemic meanings and which have deontic meanings? Do any examples seem to be neither epistemic nor deontic?

1. They may use the Library provided they bring a letter from their Head of Department.
2. They may be using the Library next week. It depends when they finish their report.
3. She might accept their offer of a Readership.
4. The Librarian said they might use the Library if they were very careful.
5. You can hand the essay in on Monday.
6. They can be here in ten minutes/any minute.
7. They could be here in ten minutes/any minute.
8. You mustn't touch the ornaments.
9. You mustn't be going on the ski trip. (If you were going, you would have had your confirmation last week.)
10. They can't be going to admit any more spectators.
11. You must spend your money on clothes. (Your wardrobe is choc-a-bloc.)
12. You must spend your money on clothes. (Your wardrobe is empty. What are you going to wear for your interview?)

objects, because an indirect object noun cannot always occur immediately to the right of the verb, as shown by (23).

(23) a. *The experts attributed Raphael this picture.
      b. *I forwarded Winifred the letter.
      c. *The manager presented the foreman a gold watch.
      d. *Kick John the ball.
      e. *Monica hit Martina the ball.
      f. *The critics ascribe Shakespeare this play.

The particular examples in (23) have been tested on many classes of students at all levels. Some have accepted some of the examples, especially (23b), but the vast majority have not accepted any of them.

Other evidence that attacks any clear distinction between indirect objects and adverbs of direction is presented in (24)–(25), which illustrate certain syntactic patterns common to indirect objects and adverbs of direction. The first shared property is that both can occur in WH interrogatives with the preposition *to* at the end or beginning of the clause.

(24) a. Who did John send a book to?
      b. To whom did John send a book?
(25) a. What place did you travel to?
      b. To what place did you travel?

Another property in common is that both can occur in active interrogative WH clauses with *to* omitted, but not in passive WH interrogatives.

(26) a. Who did John send the book?
      b. What place did John send the book?
(27) a. *Who was the book sent by John.
      b. *What place was the book sent by John?

Indirect objects and adverbs of direction can occur at the front of clauses preceded by *only*. In such constructions, the preposition *to* cannot be omitted – compare the indirect object in (28) and the adverb of direction in (29).

(28) a. Only to the best students would he give this book.
      b. *Only the best students would he give this book.
(29) a. Only to Glasgow would he go by train (because the service is fast).
      b. *Only Glasgow would he travel by train.

The same applies to the cleft construction in (30) and (31), where the indirect object *to the best students* in (30) and the adverb of direction *to Stromness* in (31) are preceded by *it is*.

(30) a. It is to the best students that he gives this book.
      b. *It is the best students he gives this book.
(31) a. It is to Stromness that he is going.
      b. *It is Stromness that he is going.

There is one difference (concealed by the use of *what place* in (25)): indirect objects are questioned by *who … to* or *to whom*, but adverbs of direction are questioned by *where*. However, this is one difference to be set against a number of similarities, and it could in any case be argued that the difference does not reflect a syntactic category but a difference in the sorts of entities that are the end point of the movement, *where* being reserved for places, *who* for human beings.

The analysis indicated by the above data is that we cannot maintain the traditional concept of indirect object as the *to* phrase with verbs such as *give* and *show* and that all verb complements introduced by a preposition should be treated as one category, namely oblique objects. The concept of indirect object is not dead, however. Some traditional analyses applied it to, for example, the phrase *to Harriet* in (32) and to the phrase *Harriet* in (33).

(32) Emma gave advice to Harriet.
(33) Emma gave Harriet advice.

The label 'indirect object' is useful for *Harriet* in (33). It can be declared to reflect the fact that while *Harriet* is an object – compare *Harriet was given advice by Emma* – it is felt by many analysts to be less of a direct object than *advice*, even though *advice* in (33) is not next to the verb.

Summary

Three major relationships hold between verbs and their complement nouns (and noun phrases) – subject, direct object and oblique object. There are languages in which the concept of subject cannot be easily applied, but in many languages one noun, the grammatical subject, is closely linked to the verb in a clause. The subject noun and the verb are linked in number (in English) and in person and number in other languages. The subject noun controls the interpretation of infinitives and reflexive pronouns; in *Emma wanted to help Harriet*, *help* is traditionally described as having an understood subject which is identical with the subject of *wanted*, namely *Emma*. In *Emma despised herself*, the reflexive pronoun *herself* is interpreted as referring to Emma. Grammatical subject nouns typically, though not always, denote Agents and they are typically first in clauses, thereby being the starting point of the messages conveyed. Direct object nouns, in English, immediately follow the verb in the active declarative construction and correspond to the grammatical subject of passive clauses – *Fiona phoned John* vs *John was phoned by Fiona.* In languages with sets of case suffixes (see Chapter 12), grammatical subject nouns take one set of case suffixes and direct object nouns another. In Indo-European languages, these are nominative for subject and accusative for direct object. Oblique objects are nouns that are complement to a preposition, as in (*spoke*) *about music* and (*sent the letter*) *to the manager.* In examples such as *gave a present to Bill*, with verbs such as GIVE, SHOW and TELL, *to Bill* was traditionally called the indirect object. Since these are very difficult to distinguish from directional phrases, the notion of indirect object has been abandoned in favour of oblique object but has been kept for the construction with three noun phrases, as in *Emma gave Harriet advice.*

Exercises

1. In the sentences below, pick out all the instances of grammatical subjects and logical subjects. To which sentences is the concept of understood subject relevant? List the properties of the sentences which exemplify the criteria for grammatical subjects.

1. Mr Weston pours Mr Woodhouse a cup of restoring gruel.
2. Mr Woodhouse is poured a cup of restoring gruel by Mr Weston.
3. Mr Weston pours the other guests glasses of his good wine.
4. The other guests were poured glasses of his good wine.
5. All the soldiers are leaving Meryton.
6. The soldiers are all leaving Meryton.
7. The young ladies like all the soldiers.
8. The young ladies like the soldiers all.
9. Mr Collins admires himself in the surface of the pond.
10. Mr D'Arcy tries to persuade Elizabeth to marry him.
11. Mr D'Arcy goes to the ball and does not dance with Elizabeth.
12. The oldest Bennet girls are both invited to Netherfield.

2. In the sentences below, pick out all the instances of direct object, indirect object and oblique object.

1. Caroline and Alice are coming with a hamper of food.
2. Caroline is also bringing us a single malt.
3. Caroline cooked Alice a meal.

4. Alice was cooked a meal by Caroline.
5. Heather and Morag were both pleased with Robin's work.
6. Ethel sent Fiona her history of the department.
7. The staff were all sent an e-mail message by Ronnie.
8. The dog sat in front of the fire and scratched itself.
9. Who is Irene going on holiday with?
10. The dog tore up the grass.

9 Syntactic linkage

9.1 Introduction

Syntactic linkage has to do with the devices (mainly morphological) by which speakers can signal which words, phrases or clauses are linked. It is a general concept which subsumes the traditional concepts of agreement and government. As we will see, the traditional distinction does not sit easily with the analysis of phrases into heads and modifiers, with heads controlling the modifiers. Some parts of the traditional concepts are compatible with the view that verbs are the heads of clauses; but others are not, particularly the relationship between subject noun and verb.

This chapter contains data from languages other than English. The book deals essentially with syntax for students in English (Language) courses, and most of the examples are from English. The problem is that English clauses have minimal syntactic linkage compared with, say, Latin or Russian (not to mention the marvellously intricate systems of linkage to be found in Bantu languages, in many Native American languages and in Australian languages). Agreement and government may not be prominent in Modern English, but they are central concepts of syntax and are prominent in the syntax of many languages, including Early English. For these reasons, syntactic linkage must be included, but examples are taken from other languages as well as from English.

9.2 Agreement

Agreement is found inside noun phrases and, in some of the Indo-European languages of Europe, in the copula constructions – adjective complements of BE (and other copula verbs) agree with the subject noun. Agreement in noun phrases is exemplified in (1).

(1) Latin

    a. magnus reks
       great   king   'a/the great king'

b. magna regina
   great queen   'a/the great queen'

c. magnum oppidum
   great   town   'a/the great town'

The phrases in (1a–c) could function as subjects of clauses. *Reks* in (1a), *regina* in (1b) and *oppidum* in (1c) are said to be in the nominative case, the case being signalled by the suffixes *-s*, *-a* and *-um*. The adjective translated as 'great' consists of the stem *magn-* [as in 'magnify' – to make great] plus various suffixes, *-us*, *-a* and *-um*. Which suffix is added is controlled by the head noun. *Magna reks* is incorrect, as is *magnus regina*. The nouns in (1a–c) have singular number; different suffixes appear both on the nouns and the adjectives when they are plural, as in (2).

(2) Latin

a. magni   reges
   great   kings   '(the) great kings'

b. magnae reginae
   great   queens   '(the) great queens'

c. magna   oppida
   great   towns   '(the) great towns'

The nouns in (2) are still in the nominative case and can still function as the subjects of clauses, but they are plural and have different suffixes, and the adjectives too have different suffixes. Whether, for example, the stem *magn-* takes the suffixes *-us*, *-a*, *-i* or *-ae* depends on what type of noun it modifies, what case the noun is in and whether the noun is singular or plural. That is, the noun is the controlling word but both noun and adjective change shape, that is, change their suffixes; this is why the term 'agreement' is used. The traditional formula is that adjectives agree with nouns in number and case (and also in gender, which is discussed below.) In spite of the traditional formula, we can view the noun as governing the adjective in case and number.

Old English had similar patterns of agreement between the head noun in a noun phrase and adjectives that modified it. Consider the examples in (3).

(3) Old English

a. gōd   cyning
   (a) good   king

b. gōdu   cwēn
   (a) good queen

c. gōd scip
   (a) good ship

The nouns in (3) are in the nominative case. *Cyning* in (3a) is masculine, and *scip* in (3c) is neuter. The adjective in both examples consists of the stem *gōd*, with no suffix. *Cwēn* in (3b) is feminine, and the adjective takes the suffix *-u*, *gōdu*. A richer pattern is observed when the head noun is plural, as in (4).

(4) a. gōde   cyningas
        good   kings

     b. gōda   cwēna
        good   queens

     c. gōdu   scipu
        good   ships

The masculine plural noun *cyningas* in (4a) is modified by *gōde* with the suffix *-e*. The feminine plural noun *cwēna* in (4b) is modified by *gōda*, with the suffix *-a*. Finally, in (4c) the neuter plural noun *scipu* is modified by *gōdu*, with the suffix *-u*. Although the adjective and noun in (3a) and (3b) do not change their shape, since no suffixes are added to the stem, all the nouns and adjectives in (4) do change their shape, since suffixes are added to both adjective and noun. Looking at the overall pattern for singular and plural, and for other cases, we can justifiably speak of adjective and noun agreeing in Old English.

9.3 Government

Consider now the examples in (5).

(5) Latin

     a. Servus magnum regem occidit
        slave   great   king   killed
        'A/the slave killed a/the great king'

     b. Servus magnos reges occidit
        slave   great   kings killed
        'A/the slave killed (the) great kings'

     c. Servus magnam reginam occidit
        slave   great   queen   killed
        'A/the slave killed a/the great queen'

Regem in (5a) is the direct object of *occidit* and has the suffix *-em*. The adjective has the suffix -*um*. In (5b) *reges* is the direct object of *occidit*, is plural and has the suffix -*es*. The adjective has the suffix -*os*. In (5c), *reginam* is the direct object of *occidit*, is singular and has the suffix -*am*. The adjective has the same suffix. *Regem*, *reginam* and *reges* are said to be in the accusative case. Note that *reges*, with the same suffix -*es*, is subject in (2a) and direct object in (5b), but that the adjective has different suffixes.

Occidit is a verb that requires an object in what is called the accusative case. In the examples in (5), *occidit*, in the traditional formula, governs its object noun in the accusative case; that is, it assigns accusative case to the stems *reg-* (king) and *regin-* (queen). Independently of the verb, these nouns are singular in (5a) and (5c) and plural in (5b). The combination of accusative and singular requires the choice of the suffixes -*em* or -*am* depending on the stem, and the choice of accusative and plural requires -*es* for the stem *reg-*. The properties 'accusative' and 'singular' or 'accusative and plural' are passed on to the adjective in the direct object noun phrase, *magn-*, and the appropriate suffix is chosen.

The majority of verbs in Latin assign accusative case to their object noun, but many verbs assign one or other of the remaining three cases. For example, the verb *utor* (I use) governs its object noun in the ablative case, as shown in (6).

(6) a. Reks gladium ponit
          king sword is-putting-down
          'The king is putting down the sword'

     b. Reks gladio utitur
          king sword is-using
          'The king is using the sword'

For verb and object noun too, a similar pattern occurs in Old English, as demonstrated in (7).

(7) a. se eorl slōg gōdne cyning
          that warrior killed (a)-good king

     b. se eorl slōg gode cwēne
          that warrior killed (a)-good queen

In (7b), the object noun *cwēne*, with the suffix -*e*, is modified by the adjective *gōde*, with the suffixe -*e*. This contrasts with the subject noun *cwēn* in (3b) with no suffix and modified by the adjective *gōdu*, with the suffix -*u*. In (7a), the noun *cyning* has no suffix but the adjective does have a special suffix, namely -*ne* as in *gōdne*. There is no contrast in the suffixes added to subject and object plural nouns.

The patterns of suffixes are summed up by saying that *slōg* requires its object noun to be in the accusative case. Other verbs require their noun to be in a different case; *andwyrdan* 'answer', for instance, requires its object noun to take dative suffixes, as shown in (8).

(8) se   eorl   andwyrde gōdum   cyninge
    that warrior answered (a)-good king

Cyninge in (8) has the dative case suffix -*e* and *gōdum* has the dative suffix -*um*. The verb *bīdan* 'wait for' requires its object noun to take a genitive suffix, as in (9).

(9) se   eorl   bād   gōdes   cyninges
    that warrior waited-for (a)-good king

In (9), *cyninges* has the genitive suffix -*es* and the adjective *gōdes* has the same suffix.

Prepositions in Latin also assign case to their complement nouns. *Ad* (to) governs nouns in the accusative case, and *de* (from) governs nouns in the ablative case.

The nominative case was thought of as the case that was used when speakers were using nouns to name entities. The theory was, and indeed still is, that speakers pick out and name an entity and then say something about it. (See Chapter 8 on grammatical functions.) 'Accusative' looks as though it should have something to do with accusing; this does not make much sense but results from a mistranslation into Latin of a Greek term meaning 'what is effected or brought about'. It seems that the central examples of accusative case were taken to be the Classical Greek equivalents of 'She built a house'.

'Ablative' derives from a Latin word meaning 'taking away' and occurs with prepositions expressing movement from or off something, as in (10b).

(10) a. ad hortum
        to garden   'to the garden'

     b. e   horto
        out-of garden   'out of the garden'

The above Latin examples show that different case-number suffixes are added to nouns and adjectives and that which suffix is chosen in a particular clause depends on the noun. Latin nouns fall into a number of different classes, known as genders. Gender will not be discussed here but will be examined in Chapter 12 on grammar and semantics.

Prepositions in Old English also require their complement nouns to have particular case suffixes. For example, *tō* 'to' governs its complement noun in the dative case (like most prepositions), but *þurh* 'by means of' governs its complement noun in the accusative case. The distinction is exemplified in (11).

(11) a. tō þǣm cyninge
          to that king

      b. þurh   þone cyning
          by-means-of that   king

In (11a), *þǣm* is the dative form of *se* 'that' and *cyninge* has the dative suffix *-e*. In (11b), *þone* is the accusative form of *se* but *cyning* has no suffix.

9.4 Number and person linkage

We turn now to the final strand of syntactic linkage in Latin, the relationship between subject nouns and verbs. Consider (12).

(12) Latin

      a. reks   legit
          the-king is-reading

      b. reges   legunt
          the-kings are-reading

In (12a), *reks* is singular and the verb *leg-* (read) has the suffix *-it*, which is singular. In (12b), *reges* is plural and *leg-* has the suffix *-unt*, which is plural. The traditional formula is that the verb agrees with the subject noun in number (and person). This analysis accords with the view that the subject noun (phrase) is more important than the other nouns in a clause because speakers use subject nouns to name the entity they want to talk about. At various places in this introduction, however, we have seen that there are good reasons to consider the verb the head of a given clause, controlling all the other words and phrases in it. From the perspective of dependency relations (Chapter 1) and the lexicon (Chapter 5), the relation between the verb and subject noun is no different from the relations between the verb and other nouns in clauses.

Whichever analysis readers favour, the term 'agreement in number' is not accurate. Either the subject noun imposes a given number on the verb or the verb imposes a given number of the noun. That is, both analyses recognise a controlling word, and where there is a controlling word we are dealing with government.

Verbs in Latin signal more than just number. Other suffixes are added to verb stems in Latin, as shown in (13).

(13) Latin

    a. epistolam lego
       letter   I-am-reading   'I am reading the/a letter'

    b. epistolam legis
       letter   you (sg)-are-reading
       'You (singular) are reading the/a letter'

    c. epistolam legimus
       letter   we-are-reading   'We are reading the/a letter'

The contrast between *lego* in (13a) and *legis* in (13b) has to do with who is presented as reading, the speaker or the addressee. The speaker is considered the central participant in a conversation, the first person. The addressee is the second in importance, that is, is the second person. The speaker and others can be presented as jointly doing something, as in (13c). *Lego* is described as being in the first person singular, *legimus* as being in the first person plural and *legis* as being in the second person singular. In (12a, b), the speaker presents the action as being performed by neither the speaker nor the hearer but by a third person in (12a) and by third persons in (12b). *Legit* is said to be in the third person singular, and *legunt* is described as being in the third person plural. Latin has pronouns, but they were not used unless for emphasis.

9.5 Syntactic linkage in English

Syntactic linkage in English is less complex than in Latin for the simple reason that English nouns no longer have a case system like the Latin one and English verbs have only one contrast in person and number. English uses word order and prepositions to signal syntactic links. As discussed in Chapter 8 on grammatical functions, in the active, declarative construction the subject and object nouns are never preceded by prepositions, the subject noun is immediately to the left of the verb (allowing for modifiers such as relative clauses) and the direct object noun is immediately to the right of the verb. Adjectives modifying a given noun are immediately to its left. Compare the word order in the line of Latin poetry in (14) and the word order in the English translation.

(14) Latin

    Cerberus et   nullas hodie petat   improbus umbras
    Cerberus and no   today let-him-seek voracious shadows
    'Let voracious Cerberus seek no shadows today' (Propertius)

The adjective *improbus*, the second last word in the clause, modifies the first word, *Cerberus*, and the adjective *nullas*, the third word in the clause, modifies the last word, *umbras*. (Note that (14) is a line of poetry; native speakers of Latin, as far as we can make out, did not talk off the cuff in this complex fashion.) In the English translation, *voracious* immediately precedes *Cerberus* and *no* immediately precedes *shadows*. English pronouns have retained some case distinctions, and these are relevant to syntactic linkage. In standard (written) English, *I, we, he, she* and *they* occur as subject and *me, us, him, her* and *them* occur as direct, indirect or oblique object. A couple of examples are given in (15).

(15) a. He told her the whole story.
      b. She told him the whole story.

The construction in (16) – called the [CONTRAST] construction in Chapter 3 – does have an unusual word order in that the direct object or oblique object phrase is put at the front of the clause.

(16) a. The other plan she rejected out of hand.
      b. To her eldest son she left the Aubusson tapestries.

The entire object phrase is moved to the front of the clause, that is, the noun and all its modifiers. The noun and its modifiers are next to each other but the whole noun phrase is in an unusual position in the clause. Relative clauses and noun complement clauses (see Chapters 6 and 7 on clauses) can and do occur separated from their head noun, as in (17).

(17) a. The vase got broken that Sheila had brought all the way from Chengdu.
      b. The plan was rejected out of hand that traffic should be banned.
      c. The idea dismayed the Prime Minister that the Dome was dull.

In (17a), the relative clause *that Sheila had brought all the way from Chengdu* is separated from its head noun *vase* by the phrase *got broken*. *The vase got broken* is an intransitive construction and there is no other noun that might be taken for the head modified by the relative clause. Noun complement clauses can be separated from the noun they modify even in transitive clauses. Example (17b) poses no problem because it is intransitive and the noun complement clause *that traffic should be banned* can only be interpreted as modifying *plan*. In (17c), which reads much more awkwardly than (17b) but is nonetheless acceptable, the noun complement clause *that the Dome was dull* relates to the content of an idea, plan, proposal, theory and so on and can only be interpreted as modifying *idea*. (Noun complement clauses always relate to the content of an idea and so on; this is one of the criteria by which you can decide

whether a given clause is a noun complement or a relative clause.) In general, then, phrases in English can be separated from the word they modify and so can clauses, but modifier words are not separated from their head word.

English has a minimal amount of linkage between subject noun and verb. Only the verb BE has any linkage in the past tense, *was* requiring a singular noun and *were* requiring a plural noun (in standard English). All other verbs have one past-tense form (and are said to be invariable in the past tense). In the present tense, BE is again idiosyncratic; it has a first person singular form *am* in addition to the contrast between *is* (third person, singular) and *are* (second person singular and all persons plural). Apart from the modal verbs such as CAN, MUST and so on, which are invariable, all other verbs take the suffix -*s* in the third person singular – *The dog barks* vs *The dogs bark.*

9.6 Number in English

The person-number relationship between subject verb and noun in English is simple compared with the large number of suffixes in Latin, yet the English system is not straightforward. One complexity is that while we are here focusing on the verb system in standard English, most of the population of the UK *speak* some non-standard variety. Many non-standard varieties differ from the standard one; in some, speakers have generalised the -*s* suffix to all persons – *We sits quietly in the classroom, you knows what I'm talking about,* while in others the speakers have removed the -*s* suffix – *She live in that street.*

Even speakers of standard English itself disagree over whether a singular or plural verb should be used with certain nouns. For instance, *committee* is a singular noun but is used to refer to groups of more than one person. Many speakers and writers use either a singular or a plural verb depending on whether they view a particular committee as several people or as a single unit. *The committee are discussing this proposal today* presents the committee as several individuals who have to discuss the matter and work out a decision. *The committee is discussing the proposal today* presents the committee in a more impersonal manner, as a single unit. Every generation, however, appears to contain speakers who believe that if a noun is singular the verb should always be singular. Such speakers are becoming rarer.

9.7 Gender in English

Nouns in English do not fall into different grammatical classes of the sort found in Latin. As we have seen in the discussion in Chapter 5 on the lexicon, English nouns do split up into classes, but the split is not unrelated to the meaning and is not reflected in syntactic linkage. Consider the examples in (18).

(18) a. My sister phoned. She said that the children were back at school.
b. Your brother went out. He said he was going to the bank.
c. The car is ready. It just needed new points.

The pronoun *she* is used in reference to a female, *he* in reference to a male and *it* in reference to an entity that is neither male nor female. In contrast, there is no obvious reason why the Latin noun *mensa* (table) is said to have feminine gender, nor why *hortus* (garden) is labelled 'masculine' and *oppidum* (town) is labelled 'neuter'. Despite the simplicity of the (typical) examples in (18), English usage is not without its subtleties. It is said that some speakers of English refer to cars and boats as though they were female, as in *She's a wonderful car*, but this usage appears to be falling into disuse.

Reference to babies and animals varies. Parents of a baby and owners of, in particular, cats and dogs, know the sex of their child or animal and use *he* or *she*. Speakers who do not know the identity of a particular baby often refer to the baby by *it* (indeed I was about to write 'often refer to it'). The choice of *it* is usually caused by lack of knowledge; once particular babies have been introduced as Selena or Rachel, Angus or Torquil, they will thereafter be referred to by *he* or *she* as appropriate. But just to demonstrate that context is important, parents can be observed referring to their baby by *it*, a usage that typically expresses love for the baby.

Similarly, the choice of pronouns for animals is affected by the use of proper names. Example (19a) is perfectly normal, (19b) is peculiar.

(19) a. The dog slunk under the table. It had eaten the sandwiches.
b. Towser slunk under the table. He (??it) had eaten the sandwiches.

We close this chapter with a reminder that the relations implicated in syntactic linkage are dependency relations holding between heads and modifiers. Some relations cross clause boundaries (especially the boundaries of relative clauses), but mostly they hold within single clauses.

Summary

Many languages have devices which signal which words belong together as head and modifiers; that is, they signal syntactic linkage. Traditionally,

two types of devices are recognised, namely agreement and government. Agreement was applied to examples in which a head and its modifier were both marked for some property. In many languages, the head noun in a noun phrase and the adjectives that modify it all carry markings for case and number, while the subject noun in a clause and the verb both carry markings for person and number. Government was applied in constructions in which the head was not marked but the modifier was. For example, in many languages the direct object of a verb carries a particular case suffix but the verb itself has no marking. Likewise, in prepositional phrases the complement of the preposition has a case suffix but the preposition itself has no marking. In spite of the traditional distinction, instances of agreement and government all involve a head assigning some property or properties to its modifiers. The current preferred view is that all syntactic linkage is government.

Exercises

1. Consider the following Latin sentences, paying attention to the incorrect ones (marked with an asterisk) as well as to the correct ones. What do the examples tell you about the linkage between nouns and adjectives in Latin and about the relationship between verb and subject noun?

1. Agricola magnum/parvum gregem agit
   farmer large/small   flock   is-driving
   The farmer is driving a large/small flock.

2. Agricola parvam/magnam carrucam agit
   farmer small/large   carriage is-driving
   The farmer is driving a small/big carriage.

   [*Agricola magnum/parvum carrucam agit,
   *Agricola magnam/parvam gregem agit]

3. Carruca parva est
   carriage small is
   The carriage is small.

4. Greks magnus est
   flock big   is
   The flock is big.

5. Oppidum magnum est
   town   big   is
   The town is big.

[*Carruca parvus/parvum est, *Greks magna/magnum est,
*Oppidum magna/magnus est]

6. Romani magnum oppidum constituunt
   Romans large   town   are-building
   The Romans are building a large town.

7. Agricola magnam villam constituit
   Farmer big   villa   is-building
   The farmer is building a big villa.

[*Romani magnum oppidum constituit,
*Agricola magnam villam constituunt]

2. The examples below are taken from an account of the language of
speakers in Reading. Analyse the system of agreement between the verb
and the subject NP. Pay particular attention to the verbs DO and HAVE.

1. I grabs hold of him and legs it up Blagdon Hill.
2. We buses it down the town.
3. You knows my sister, the one who's small.
4. They calls me all the names under the sun, don't they?
5. Well, I have got a boyfriend.
6. We does things at school with tape recorders.
7. We has a little fire, keeps us warm.
8. Well, how much do he want for it?
9. That's what I does anyway, I just ignores them.
10. She cadges, she do.
11. He said, why have you been away?
12. Sometimes on Saturdays I has to stop in.
13. Your dad do play cricket though don't he?
14. But it hurts my dad more than it do her.
15. He don't want to look at your ugly face.
16. I fancies going over Caversham.
17. I wants to kill animals.
18. I knows how to stick in the boot.

10 Heads and modifiers revisited

10.1 For and against verb phrases

In this short chapter, we pick up additional topics to do with dependency relations and constituent structure. The outcome of our earlier discussion was that every phrase has a central word which controls the other words, phrases and even clauses that occur in it. The central word is the head and the other words and phrases are its modifiers, which typically occur next to their head. Such phrases 'move around' together, can be replaced by a single word and can be ellipted. These points are illustrated in (1).

(1) The Ethel that we knew and loved has left – just packed her bags and walked out.

As a proper noun, *Ethel* typically does not allow the definite article *the*. Proper nouns do allow definite articles, however, provided they are also modified by a relative clause. Presumably the speaker who utters (1) is thinking of Ethel not as a single individual but as a bundle of individuals or personae who appear and disappear depending on the situation. The phrase *the Ethel that we knew and loved* picks out one of these individuals (as opposed, say, to *the Ethel that ate administrative staff for breakfast*). In the lexicon, we must include information about the subcategorisation of proper nouns, that they do allow a definite article but only along with a relative clause. *Ethel* is the head of the noun phrase *the Ethel that we knew and loved*; inside the noun phrase, it controls the occurrence of the word *the* and the relative clause *that we knew and loved*.

That whole sequence of words can be replaced by the single word *she*. The phenomenon of ellipsis is shown in the second clause *just packed her bags and left*. This clause has no subject; if there were one, it would be *she* or *the Ethel that we knew and loved*. Either the long sequence of words is replaced by a pronoun or it is ellipted, as in the second clause above.

In Chapter 1, we looked at examples of noun phrases, prepositional phrases – *in the garden*, adjective phrases – *very difficult*, and adverb

113

phrases – *amazingly quickly.* In Chapter 5 on the lexicon, we adopted the idea that the verb is the head of the clause and controls all the other constituents in the clause, including the subject noun, which we treated as a complement of the verb. Many descriptions of English use a type of phrase known as the verb phrase. In (1), the subject noun phrase is *The Ethel that we knew and loved* and the verb phrase would be *has left.* Other descriptions of English do not recognise verb phrases (and in many languages other than English the concept of verb phrase is not obviously applicable).

The difficulty is that the criteria for recognising phrases do not apply straightforwardly to English clauses. The strongest criteria are trans-position and substitution. For all other types of phrase, these criteria apply without difficulty inside clauses and in common constructions – see Chapter 2. But they do not apply to sequences of finite verb plus object(s) of some kind. It used to be thought that the occurrence of *do so* counted as a criterion. An example is in (2).

(2) Norman Lemming jumped off the cliff and William Lemming did so too.

Did so indeed substitutes for *jumped off the cliff,* but two words are involved, and it seems clear that the verb *did* substitutes for *jumped* and that *so* substitutes for the complements of *jumped.* Example (2) is the sort of example that turns up in discussions of American linguists, but it is not the normal construction in British English, where (3) is the common construction. In (3), the sequence is *so did,* which is not even a straight-forward substitution of *did* for *jumped* and *so* for *off the cliff* because the verb and its complement would have to be transposed to yield *so did.*

(3) Norman Lemming jumped off the cliff and so did William Lemming.

The one structure from spontaneous spoken English that might fit is shown in (4).

(4) Came right in he did without so much as a knock.

Unfortunately, the structure of (4) is not clear. *Came right in he did* could be seen as a rearrangement of *He did come right in,* except that in the latter *come* has no tense, whereas in (4) *came* is past tense. Moreover, new electronic bodies of spoken English are yielding examples such as *They complained about it all the time they did* which has two clauses, *They complained about it all the time* and the tagged-on clause *they did.* So (4) can be analysed as having a two-clause structure in which the first clause, as happens regularly in spontaneous speech, is lacking a subject. That is, (4) is not a basic construction but results from ellipsis.

Other arguments for verb phrases turn on examples of the sort in (5) and (6).

(5) Harriet couldn't marry Mr Knightley but Emma could.

(6) What Harriet did was marry Mr Martin.

The argument is that in (5) the phrase *marry Mr Knightley* has been ellipted – *Emma could marry Mr Knightley* is reduced to *could*. In (6), *was* has the WH clause *What Harriet did* as its subject and *marry Mr Knightley* as its complement. That is, the sequence *marry Mr Knightley* turns up in different slots, and in (6) can even be genuinely transposed to the front to give (7).

(7) Marry Mr Martin was what Harriet did.

These examples show that a verb plus complements (and adjuncts) does form a phrase in certain constructions, but the argument does not apply to *has left* in (1), with a verb marked for tense. Only verbs without tense and aspect turn up freely in different constructions. One piece of data that looks more promising for verb phrases is conjunction, as in (8).

(8) Emma insulted Miss Bates and annoyed Mr Knightley.

Example (8) can be analysed as having a subject noun phrase, *Emma*, and two phrases – verb phrases – connected by *and*: *insulted Miss Bates* and *annoyed Mr Knightley*. There are, however, alternative analyses that treat the supposed verb phrases as clauses whose subject noun phrase has been ellipted, and other analyses try to handle conjunction in terms of heads and their dependent modifiers rather than in terms of phrases. Although many analyses employ verb phrases, the evidence is much weaker than for other types of phrase and not strong enough for us to abandon the view that the verb is the head of the clause.

10.2 Verb, core, nucleus and periphery

Descriptions that focus on dependency relations do not devote much time to the arguments for and against verb phrases. They incorporate the view that other divisions of the clause, based on dependencies, are more important. Clauses are analysed as having a nucleus and a periphery. The nucleus contains the verb and its complements (subject, direct object, indirect object and oblique objects/adverbs of direction); the periphery consists of oblique objects which are adverbs of time or adverbs of location, and some other types of adverb. (Adverbs are a very large and heterogeneous class, and in at least one construction – the middle construction – adverbs of manner seem to be obligatory with some verbs; for example, *Her new book reads well* is quite acceptable but *Her new book reads* is not acceptable.)

The split between nucleus and periphery is sometimes replaced by a three-way split between core, nucleus and periphery. The core of a clause is the verb, the nucleus is the verb plus complements as described above, and the periphery is also as described above. The idea that the verb in a clause is the core fits with other properties of verbs. We saw in Chapter 1 on dependencies that the verb in a clause can be regarded as controlling the other constituents. This view provides an elegant way of handling the relationships that are the concern of the lexicon or dictionary, as explained in Chapter 5.

A final and strong piece of evidence for the core position of verbs in clauses comes from languages in which a clause can consist of a single verb. Examples are given in (9)–(11).

(9) Latin

    a. pugnatur
       was-fought   'There was fighting'

    b. tonuit
       thundered   'There was thunder'

(10) Turkish

    konuş ul   maz [one word]
    spoken Passive Negative   'It is not spoken', i.e. 'No speaking'

(11) Luganda (Africa – Bantu language)

    a li   gi goba [one word]
    she Future it chase   'She will chase it' (a chicken)

The Latin clause in (9a) consists of the verb *pugnatur*. This verb is passive; while it might be thought that a subject noun phrase has been ellipted, it is difficult to know what that noun phrase might be. The same applies to the Turkish passive verb in (10). The Luganda verb in (11) is active. No independent noun phrases are needed because in context the person doing the chasing and the bird being chased are obvious to the hearer.

10.3 What is the head of a noun phrase?

Questions can be asked about the traditional view of nouns as the head of noun phrases. It remains true that the noun controls the other constituents in noun phrases but particular problems affect noun phrases. Consider first the pairs of examples in (12)–(14).

(12) a. Harriet swooned.
      b. Harriet admired Mr Knightley.

(13) a. Willoughby ran up (to where he had seen Marianne and Margaret).
      b. Willoughby ran up the hill (to where he had seen Marianne and Margaret).

(14) a. The book is boring.
      b. The book is astonishingly boring.
      c. the boring book
      d. the astonishingly boring book

Examples (12a, b) show that a verb or a verb and its modifiers occur in the same slot in a clause. Examples (13a, b) show that a preposition or a preposition and its complement occur in the same slot. Examples (14a–d) show that an adjective or an adjective and its modifiers occur in the same slot, whether as complement of *is* or modifying a noun. In other words, the entire phrase occurs in the same slots in clauses as the head word. (Looking at where particular types of word or types of phrase are to be found in phrases, clauses and sentences is not unlike botanists, say, searching for specimens of a particular plant and plotting on maps where the plant grows. The botanists are said to be studying the geographical distribution of the plant, its distribution over the country; similarly, linguists talk of studying the distribution of words and phrases over phrases, clauses and sentences, not to mention larger texts, studied in discourse analysis. Having said all that, we can now provide the technical way of putting it: the head of a phrase and the phrase itself have the same distribution.)

The above does not apply to all nouns. It applies to proper nouns, which normally do not allow modifiers – but see (15b, c) below.

(15) a. Ethel wishes to ask you some awkward questions.
      b. The Ethel we all know and love wishes to ask you some awkward questions.
      c. Ethel with the in-your-face turn of phrase wishes to ask you some awkward questions.

Examples (15a–c) tell us something about the noun phrases that occur followed by a phrase such as *wishes to ask you some awkward questions*. To introduce the technical way of putting it, linguists talk of words and phrases occurring in frames or environments. In the frame or environment ___ *wishes to ask you some awkward questions* we find either the head noun *Ethel* on its own, as in (15a), or the example discussed above in which *Ethel* is modified by a definite article and a relative clause – (15b), or *Ethel*, not modified by a definite article but only by a prepositional phrase, as in (15c).

Plural nouns such as *golfers* likewise have the same distribution as any phrases of which they are head, as shown by (16).

(16) a. Golfers can be good company.
      b. Enthusiastic golfers with large handicaps can be good company.
      c. These enthusiastic golfers that I met at the nineteenth hole can be good company.

In the environment ___ *can be good company* we find *golfers* on its own, as in (16a); we find *enthusiastic golfers with large handicaps*, as in (16b) – that is, the head noun modified by an adjective and a prepositional phrase; and we find *these enthusiastic golfers that I met at the nineteenth hole*, as in (16c) – that is, the head noun *golfers* modified by the demonstrative *these* and a relative clause. Analogous examples can be produced for singular mass nouns such as *sand* or *flour*.

The phrases that do not conform to the above patterns are those containing singular count nouns such as *golfer*, which cannot occur on its own but requires an article or demonstrative as shown by (17). (*Golfer* in (17a) and (17d) is not a nickname. If it were, it would be a proper noun and (17a) would be acceptable.)

(17) a. *Golfer has a pretty powerful swing.
      b. The/this/a golfer has a pretty powerful swing.
      c. The/a golfer who is in training has a pretty powerful swing.
      d. *Golfer who is in training has a pretty powerful swing.

Many analysts have responded to the above pattern of distribution by suggesting that what we have been calling noun phrases in (17a–d) do not have nouns as their heads. Instead, they propose that the determiner is the head and that the phrases should be called determiner phrases. Phrases containing proper nouns or plural nouns or singular mass nouns are to be analysed as determiner phrases containing a determiner that happens to be zero. This approach makes it attractive to recognise two types of head: syntactic heads that control the distribution of phrases and determines their type – determiner, adjective, prepositional phrase and so on, and semantic heads that control the sort of complements and adjectives that can occur. In an introductory textbook, we do not need to choose between one or the other approach; the fact remains that dependency relations are central to syntactic structure.

11 Roles

11.1 Roles, grammar and meaning

Why discuss roles? The first part of the reply is that concepts such as Agent, Patient, Instrument and so on are regularly used in accounts of the active and passive constructions, of prepositions in English and of prepositions and case suffixes in other languages, and with respect to various syntactic structures. It is essential to understand the difficulties in defining roles and to be aware of what counts as good practice in this area of grammar. The second part of the reply is that the concept of roles has never failed to elicit an immediate interested response from students. To use a colloquial phrase, it rings a bell and deserves to be explored. The third part of the reply is that roles are used in descriptions of many languages other than English.

We saw in Chapter 6 on clauses that clauses denote situations. Situations are analysed as consisting of a state or event (see the discussion of aspect in Chapter 13) in which certain types of participants take part. There are central participants, such as Agent and Patient, and peripheral participants (which some analysts call '**circumstances**') such as Place and Time. The distinction between the central participants and the peripheral circumstances largely corresponds to the distinction between the core of a clause and the periphery of a clause (as discussed in Chapter 3). In Chapter 3, we mentioned a further distinction between the nucleus and core of a clause, the nucleus being a verb or BE plus an adjective, say. The nucleus corresponds to the state or event at the centre of any situation.

Let us look briefly at some examples illustrating how we can put roles to work. They can be used in the analysis of constructions that have the same syntactic structure but different sets of roles. Consider (1) and (2).

(1) a. Memo ate the spaghetti.
    b. Memo liked lasagna.
(2) a. Emma made Harriet her friend.
    b. Emma made Harriet some food.

In the situation denoted by (1a), Memo is involved in an action, but not in the situation denoted by (1b); he has different roles, although in both *Memo* is the subject. In the situation described by (2a), Emma does something to Harriet, whereas in (2b) Emma does something for Harriet. Again, Harriet plays different roles although *Harriet* is the indirect object in both examples – indirect object as defined at the end of Chapter 8.

NPs can be conjoined, as shown in (3). Certain restrictions apply, and examples that break the restrictions sound odd, such as (3a, b).

(3) a. The quiche and I were cooking.
    b. Erika made her mother an omelette and the kitchen a mess.

In (3a), *I* refers to an Agent, but *the quiche* does not. In (3b), *her mother* refers to the recipient of the omelette, but *the kitchen* certainly does not refer to a recipient. Coordinated NPs must have the same role.

Roles are also relevant to the neutral order of prepositions, as in (4).

(4) a. Bill went to London on Monday.
    b. Bill went on Monday to London.
    c. My brother lives near Strasbourg.
    d. Near Strasbourg my brother lives.
    e. He planted the garden with roses last November.
    f. He planted the garden last November with roses.

Example (4a) shows normal neutral word order – goal phrase *to London* followed by time phrase *on Monday*. The reverse order in (4b) is not neutral, and is even peculiar out of context. The key point is that, since all the phrases are prepositional phrases, there is no difference in constituent structure. What is different is the role attaching to the NP in the prepositional phrase.

Example (4c) shows the neutral order with a verb such as *live* – location phrase at the end of the clause. Example (4d) has the location phrase at the front of the clause, which is not neutral order and could only be used if another speaker had used the phrase *near Strasbourg* and the speaker of (4d) picked up the phrase and emphasised it. Examples (4e) and (4f) are parallel to (4a) and (4b); note that *last November* can be moved to the front of the clause but moving *with roses* to the front of the clause produces a very peculiar example.

11.2 Criteria for roles

A major question is how we decide how many roles are needed in the analysis of a given language. The central point is that, while intuitions may be the starting point of the analysis, the central criteria are gram-

matical (syntactic or morphological) or question–answer pairs such as those used below. A participant role that is not supported by grammatical criteria is suspicious. We do not deny appeal to intuitions nor the fact that for a given language some speakers will agree some of the time about some intuitions. But intuitions are not infallible, are not always shared and do need to be justified by evidence.

Another important point that must be mentioned here is that grammatical evidence allows only very general distinctions of meaning to be made. We will find ourselves working with very general roles, but the interpretation of any given clause combines information from the syntactic structure, including roles, information from the lexical verb and information from the lexical nouns inserted into a given structure. (See the discussion of syntactic structure and the lexicon in Chapter 5.) In the discussion that follows, roles are treated as assigned to nouns; since nouns are the heads of noun phrases, the property of being an Agent or Patient, say, spreads from nouns to the noun phrases that they head.

We begin with the simplest sort of example, as in (5)–(6).

(5) The baby chewed the biscuit.
(6) The baby is heavy.

In (5), *baby* is an Agent and *biscuit* is a Patient. Since it is not so obvious what role is to be assigned to *baby* in (6), we will leave the role undecided for the moment. What is important is that there are tests in English that distinguish the constructions in (5) and (6): (5), but not (6), is an appropriate answer to the question in (7).

(7) What happened?

The above question enables us to sort out events from states, since only sentences describing events can answer the question *What happened?* The questions in (8) and (9) pick out Agent and Patient.

(8) What did X do?
(9) What happened to X?

In (8), X can be replaced by *the baby*: *What did the baby do? He/she chewed the biscuit.* In (9), X can be replaced by *the biscuit*: *What happened to the biscuit? The baby chewed it.* Example (6) is not an appropriate answer to either (8) or (9).

Other tests for Agent are available in English. One test is whether a clause can be incorporated into the WH cleft construction *What X did was/What X is doing is* and so on. For example, (5) can be incorporated in the construction to yield (10).

(10)   What the baby did was chew the biscuit.

Other tests are whether the verb in a given clause can be put into the progressive or into the imperative. Example (5) meets both of these criteria, as shown in (11) and (12).

(11)   The baby was chewing the biscuit.
(12)   Chew the biscuit!

These tests are weaker because they are also met by verbs that denote states: *The patient is suffering a lot of pain, You will soon be owning all the land round here.* (The last example is from a TV play.) (Note that *The patient is suffering a lot of pain* is bizarre as an answer to *What is the patient doing?* (Compare *annoying the nurses, complaining about the food* and so on.)

Examples (13)–(15) introduce other roles.

(13)   Hartfield House is in Surrey.
(14)   Mr Knightley rode to Kingston.
(15)   Eleanor and Marianne travelled from Shropshire.

In (13), *Surrey* has the role of Place; it denotes the location of Hartfield House. In (14), *Kingston* has the role of Goal, in that it denotes the goal of Mr Knightley's journey, while in (15) *Shropshire* denotes the starting point, or source, of the journey and has the role of Source. Compare the examples in (16) and (17).

(16)   Frank gave a piano to Jane Fairfax.
(17)   Jane Fairfax received a piano from Frank.

Example (16), like (14), contains the preposition *to*. Like (14), it describes movement, in the sense that the piano moves from a shop or warehouse to beside Jane Fairfax. This parallel is captured by assigning *Jane Fairfax* the role of Goal. Of course, the movement of a possession to its owner is not exactly the same as the movement of a person or vehicle to a destination, but this does not require different roles. Different interpretations will result from the different lexical verbs and lexical nouns.

Similarly, the analogy between (15) and (17) leads us to assign the role of Source to *Frank* in (17). The sentence presents the piano as starting its journey from Frank (whether that is literally true or not), just as Eleanor and Marianne started their journey from Shropshire. The important element in the analysis is not just that we can unpack the meanings of the sentences in each pair and discover parallels, but the occurrence of the same preposition in (14) and (16), and in (15) and (17). Important too is the fact that in many languages the equivalents of (14) and (16), and (15) and (17), contain the same preposition or case affix.

Other roles are illustrated in (18)–(19).

(18) The thief smashed the window with a hammer.
(19) Captain Wentworth recovered the property for Mrs Smith.

Hammer in (18) has the self-explanatory role of Instrument, although we will argue below that Instrument is a subtype of a more general role. Instruments are signalled by *with* in English, and a contrast is possible between passive sentences such as those in (20) and (21). (Typically the Instrument role is played by inanimate objects such as hammers and saws, but it could be played by an animate being in unusual situations: *Bond smashed the window with his opponent.* The general construction and the preposition *with* impose the Instrument role; the attachment of a human noun to that role is unusual, but the properties of the noun do not force the role to change.)

(20) The window was broken with a hammer.
(21) The window was broken by a hammer.

Example (20) is appropriate to a situation in which someone has picked up the hammer and used it to break the window. The Agent is not mentioned explicitly, but the occurrence of *with* signals the Instrument status of *hammer* and the presence of an unspecified Agent. Example (21) describes a situation in which, say, the hammer is balanced on a shelf beside the window but falls off 'of its own accord' and breaks the window. There is no Agent to be specified, and (21) indeed presents the hammer as the Agent through the occurrence of *by*. In (19), *Mrs Smith* has the role known generally as Benefactive, the person who benefits from an action. Benefactive is signalled by *for*. Some analysts treat Benefactive as a subtype of Goal: this relates it to the movement phrase *head for London*.

The direct objects in (22a–c) also raise the question of extra roles.

(22) a. Wren built St Paul's Cathedral.
      b. Siobhan burnt a pattern on the piece of wood.
      c. The dog dug a hole in the lawn.

The question arises because it has been suggested that the direct object NP is not a Patient but rather a Result; this role would capture the fact that verbs such as *build* and *dig* denote actions which bring things into existence, rather than actions carried out on already existing things. It is true that the sentence *What did X do to Y?* cannot be appropriately answered by any of (22a–c). However, this is because the question can only be asked concerning things that exist already, and information in the lexical entry for *build* will specify that it relates to bringing things into existence. Moreover, 'result' noun phrases behave grammatically like Patient noun phrases; they function as direct object in active sentences; they function as subject in passive sentences. (Compare *The hole was dug in the lawn by the dog* and so on). Clauses containing 'result' noun phrases can be incorporated into WH clefts as in (10), *What the dog did was dig a hole in the lawn.* The grammatical evidence suggests that we are dealing with Patient noun phrases; the 'result' component of the meaning conveyed by (22a–c) can be derived from the meaning of the verbs BUILD, BURN and DIG, and no extra role is needed.

Another role that has been proposed is that of Theme, a role that is neutral with respect to Agent and Patient and is assigned to noun phrases such as *the vase* in (23a) and (23b).

(23) a. The vase stood on the table in the hall.
      b. Imogen took the vase to her mother's.
      c. Imogen broke the vase.

In (23b), *the vase* is the direct object of *took*. The vase does not change its state, as it does in (23c), but merely its location. This semantic difference is not reflected in any grammatical properties (or at least not major ones) and can be captured in the information in the lexical entries for *take* and *break*. The role of Theme is not necessary.

What of *vase* in (23a)? The sentence clearly does not describe an action, since it is not an answer to questions such as *What happened?* or *What was happening?* Nor does it answer questions such as *What did the vase do?* or *What happened to the vase?* (We assume that the sentence is not metaphorical and does not describe the vase taking up its stance on the table.) Example (23a) describes a state, but what role should be assigned to *vase*? By the same token, (6) describes a state too: what role is appropriate for *baby*? The grammar of English remains neutral in this respect, and we will treat *vase* in (23a) and *baby* in (6) as merely being neutral between Agent and Patient.

Certain verbs and adjectives denoting states do require a different role for subject nouns, as shown by (24).

(24) a. Sue knows the answer.
      b. The answer is known to Sue.

Example (24a) is not an answer to the question *What does Sue do?* or to the question *What is happening to Sue?* The paraphrase in (24b) shows that *to* is a possible preposition in the passive, which in turn indicates that *Sue* does not simply have the Neutral role. Many accounts of participant roles propose the role of Experiencer, the label reflecting the notion that (24a) describes a situation in which Susan has a psychological experience. We adopt **Experiencer**, particularly as in some languages with

rich systems of case (see Chapters 9 and 12) there are clear distinctions, central to the grammar, which support a contrast between Patient and Experiencer.

Verbs like *know* are called **stative verbs**. Lists of stative verbs in English usually include verbs such as *understand, like, believe, see* and *hear*, which denote psychological experiences. Adjectives such as *sorry, ashamed* and *joyful* are often included as denoting psychological experiences. The evidence from English, as in (24), is typically in the form of paraphrase relations, such as *be visible to X* for *X sees* and *be audible to X* for *X hears*.

11.3 Roles and role-players

We said above that grammatical criteria establish very broad categories. We have already seen that grammatical patterns in English establish a very general role of Patient; the differences in meaning that led analysts to propose the roles of Result and Theme arise from the meaning of specific lexical verbs and should be handled in the lexical entries for these verbs. We now look again at the role of Agent, invoking the concept of prototype that was so useful in the discussion of word classes in Chapter 4 and distinguishing clearly between roles and role-players.

It has long been demonstrated that the most reliable and general criteria for Agents – answering questions such as *What does X do?* or *What is X doing?*, completing WH clefts – *What X does is ___* and occurring in the progressive – lead to a very general concept of Agent. Prototypical Agents are human beings acting of their own volition, initiating an action, carrying it out using their own energy and producing an effect on something. *Jim* in (25) is a prototypical Agent.

(25) Jim was happily chopping logs.

Prototypical Agents allow clauses to be continued by *be at it* and to contain adverbs such as *enthusiastically* or *masterfully*, as in (26a) and (26b).

(26) a. Jim was chopping logs when Margaret left and was still at it when she got back.
b. Jim was enthusiastically chopping logs.

Some Agents meet the general criteria outlined above but achieve some goal by exerting their will-power. Consider the examples in (27).

(27) a. Captain Oates died in order to save his comrades.
b. The fugitive lay motionless in order to avoid discovery.

Verbs such as *die* and *lie* do not denote actions but can be put into the imperative, which is not a test for actions but is a test for volition: *Die a hero's death for Sparta!* and *Lie still or they will see you!* An adverb such as *accidentally* signals that an action is not voluntary, but it can occur in imperative sentences and the latter can be given an interpretation. Thus, *Kick the defender accidentally* can be taken as an instruction to kick the defender but to make it look accidental.

Some Agents do not have volition, do not initiate an action and do not expend energy. Nonetheless, they produce an effect by virtue of being in a certain position in a certain place. Example (28) is an instance of this; note that it meets the above general criteria, as demonstrated by (29).

(28) This arch supports the weight of the tower.
(29) a. What does this arch do? It supports the weight of the tower.
      b. What this arch does is support the weight of the tower.
      c. This arch is supporting the weight of the tower.

Some Agents initiate an action but do no more because they merely give a command to others to carry out some action. An example is in (30).

(30) The guard marched the prisoners round the yard.

A fourth type of Agent is conceived of as using its own energy – a living creature, a machine or a natural force. Examples are in (31).

(31) a. The computer is playing six simultaneous games of three-dimensional chess.
      b. The machine is crushing the wrecked car.
      c. The flood swept away whole villages.

The above are answers to questions such as *What is the computer doing?* and *What did the flood do?*; they fit into WH clefts – *What the computer is doing is playing six simultaneous games of three-dimensional chess* and *What the flood did was sweep away whole villages*. An extra role of Causer was proposed at one time for nouns such as *flood* in (31c). As with the other proposed extra roles, it is not required. Floods have their own non-human properties, and these are set out in the lexical entry for *flood*. Floods are simply a subtype of Agent, not prototypical but not hopelessly peripheral either.

To round off this account of roles and role-players, we will look briefly at the Instrument role and at other examples relating to the (discarded) Agent–Causer distinction. The typical instrument in this world is a tool such as a saw, hammer, screwdriver and so on, or a machine, with impromptu tools, such as lengths of wood or stones, on the periphery of the set. It is possible to imagine situations in which human beings are used as instruments: compare *Bond smashed the window with his opponent*. Of course, such situations are not normal, but they do occur from time to

time, even if mostly in novels. The crucial fact is the occurrence of *with*, signalling an Instrumental role, and the unusual nature of the particular instrument will emerge from the combination of that role with a human noun.

Finally, consider the examples in (32).

(32) a. The intense cold killed the climbers.
      b. The climbers were killed by the intense cold.
      c. The climbers were killed with the intense cold.

Cold in (32) is an Agent and has the Agent preposition *by* in (32b). In (32c) it is preceded by *with*, which is the Instrument preposition (but see below). Some entities can be involved in a causal role in some situation but can be perceived now as Agent, now as non-Agent. Again the important point is that we have to go by the grammar, and the grammar indicates that *cold* is presented as an Agent in (32b) but as a non-Agent in (32c).

The argument has been put for a broad notion of Agent based on grammatical criteria, with other details coming from the dictionary entries for individual nouns. One major criterion is that a difference in preposition indicates a difference in role, but we have not yet discussed whether all occurrences of the same preposition can be analysed as signalling the same role. Consider the sentences in (33).

(33) a. Catriona opened the door with this key.
      b. The visas are with the passports.
      c. Sally went to the party with Andrew.
      d. Alan made the loaf with strong white flour.
      e. The builders made the wall with concrete blocks.

The one noun that obviously denotes an instrument is *key* in (33a). In the situation described by (33b), the visas and the passports are in the same place – the passports are used as an orientation point for stating the whereabouts of the visas. In the situation described by (33c), Sally and Andrew are in the same place; they are together as they make their way to the party and they are together at the party. In the situations described by (33d) and (33e), the flour and the concrete blocks are perforce in the same place as the loaf and the wall, since the latter two are made out of the former. The examples in (33) have in common the notion of being in the same place, for which the term Comitative (= accompanying) is commonly used.

Returning to (33a), we should note that a person using an instrument is typically in the same place as the instrument. Examples (33a–e) all contain *with* and can all be interpreted as involving the notion of being in the same place. To this evidence can be added the fact that, in a range of languages, examples corresponding to (33a–c) employ the same case suffix. Finally, there is evidence from experiments with speakers of twelve languages from different language families that the concepts of Instrument and **Comitative** are related. We propose that *key* in (33a) is in the Comitative role and that the specific properties of *key* as denoting an instrument are set out in its lexical entry.

11.4 Problems with Patients: planting roses

We finish this chapter with a well-known and much-discussed set of examples that bear directly on participant roles and the question of whether they relate only to the objective world of the physicist or whether they also relate to the world as conceived and perceived by ordinary speakers of human languages. The examples are in (34).

(34) a. The gardener planted roses in the garden.
     b. The gardener planted the garden with roses.

Examples (34a) and (34b) are not identical in meaning. Example (34b) is true if the gardener filled the garden with rose bushes, whereas (34a) leaves it open whether the rose bushes are all over the garden or only in one part of it. If (34b) is true, (34a) is true; if (34a) is true, (34b) might or might not be true depending on the details of a particular event of planting.

The differences in meaning accompany differences in syntax; the latter make it clear that we are dealing with two different constructions. (See Chapter 3 on constructions.)

- There are differences in word order: (34a) *planted roses garden* vs (34b) *planted garden roses.*
- *Garden* is preceded by a preposition in (34a) but not (34b); *roses* is preceded by a preposition in (34b) but not (34a).
- The preposition in (34a) is *in*, but in (34b) it is *with*.
- *Roses* is the direct object of *planted* in (34a) – (34a) can be made passive, *Roses were planted in the garden by the gardener*. In (34b) the direct object is *garden*; witness the passive *The garden was planted with roses by the gardener*.

It was suggested at one time that the difference between the sentences merely had to do with whether the focus was on the roses or on the garden. Three facts make this view untenable. There is the contrast in meaning; the differences in syntax set out in (i)–(iv) above indicate

clearly that different constructions are involved. The differences extend to other constructions, as shown by (35) and (36).

(35) a. It was roses that the gardener planted in the garden.
     b. It is the garden that the gardener planted with roses.
(36) a. Roses are certain to be planted in the garden by the gardener.
     b. The garden is certain to be planted with roses by the gardener.

The (a) examples all have the same ambiguous meaning; they leave it open whether the roses fill the entire garden or are confined to one part of it. The (b) examples all have the interpretation that the garden is filled with roses. The crucial point is that the grammatical criteria show that in (34a) *roses* is the direct object; they are presented as being directly operated on by the gardener. In (34b), the garden is presented as being directly operated on by the gardener. In terms of role, *roses* in (34a) is Patient and *garden* in (34b) is Patient. Normally, the Patient in a clause is interpreted as being completely affected by the action; the *roses* are completely affected in (34a), but this tells us nothing about the garden. The *garden* is completely affected in (34b), and this gives us the essential difference in meaning from (34a). These basic differences in grammar and meaning affect (35a, b) and (36a, b).

Of course, this interpretation can be overridden by the insertion of adverbs such as *partly* – *The gardener partly planted the garden with roses* – or by a change in preposition. *The gardener planted roses in the garden* does not have the same meaning as *The gardener planted roses all over the garden*. The difference between *in* and *all over* is crucial. Similarly, *the gardener planted the garden with roses* does not have the same meaning as *The gardener partly planted the garden with roses*. However, in the absence of such adverbs, the basic interpretation stands.

Garden in the (a) examples is the complement of the preposition *in* and has to be assigned the role of Place. What role goes to *roses* in the (b) examples? Recall the discussion of (33), which concluded that in all the examples *with* has the Comitative role, based on the concept of being in the same place. Example (34b) presents the gardener as operating on the garden, causing it to be in the same place as roses. It might be objected that the English sentence *The garden is with roses* is unacceptable (though its equivalent in other languages is not), but the noun phrase *the garden with roses* is perfectly acceptable: *The garden with roses is more attractive than the garden with heathers*.

Is the difference between (34a) and (34b) really all that important, and do we need to have different roles for the two constructions? After all, no matter what the word order or preposition, when you analyse real examples of the situations described by the sentences, isn't the garden always a location and aren't the rose bushes always the things that the gardener sets in the ground? That is, shouldn't our analysis of the examples assign the Place role to *garden* and the Patient role to *roses* in both (34a) and (34b)?

The difficulty is that this alternative treatment ignores the grammatical evidence. The different meanings of (34a) and (34b) demonstrate that grammatical differences which some analysts might dismiss are actually important. We are not entitled to give preference to the presence of *partly* or to the contrast between *in* and *all over* while ignoring the contrast between *in* and *with* and a difference in grammatical function, for example *garden* as oblique object in (34a) and as direct object in (34b). We must also keep in mind that different constructions allow speakers to take different perspectives on what the physicist would treat as one and the same situation. Returning to (33e), we see that *The builders built the wall with concrete blocks* presents the concrete blocks in a Comitative role. In contrast, *The builders built the wall from/out of concrete blocks* presents the blocks as the **Source** from which the wall emerged.

We close the chapter by picking up the above mention of grammatical criteria and reminding ourselves that roles are not invented just on the basis of intuition. In addition to the grammatical criteria, one other criterion has been proposed, that there should be only one instance of a given role in a given clause – an exception being made for conjoined NPs, as in *Celia and Sally prepared a meal*. Consider, however, the example in (37).

(37)   Helen sent a scarf to Jim for Margaret.

Jim is a **Goal**. What role should be assigned to *Margaret*? Examples such as *They headed for Glasgow* and *Let's make for the island* suggest that *for* signals a Goal, but we have already decided that *to* signals a Goal. If we allow two Goals in our analysis of (37), do we fall foul of the new principle? Fortunately, we can take advantage of the distinction between core and periphery discussed in Chapter 3 on constructions. *To* phrases are complements and in the core; many verbs exclude movement phrases, and that information has to be entered in their lexical entries. With *send* the phrase *for Margaret* is optional and an adjunct, in that *for* phrases can occur with any combination of verb and other constituent: *wrote a poem for Margaret, played CDs for Margaret, learned that dance for Margaret, sat patiently for two hours for Margaret* and so on. The phrase *for Margaret* is in the periphery of the clause, and we can save our extra criterion by allowing a clause to have simultaneously a Goal phrase in its core and a Goal phrase in its periphery.

Summary

Participant roles play a useful part in the analysis of the syntax and interpretation of various constructions. Typical roles are Agent, Patient, Instrument, Place, Goal and Source. It is essential to have criteria for limiting the number of roles; a small number of very general roles can be set up on the basis of grammatical criteria. Two distinctions are fundamental. One is between roles and role-players, as in the recognition that the prototype or best central example of a player in the Agent role is a human being using his or her own energy and acting of their own volition. A peripheral example is an inanimate column without volition and not using energy. The second distinction is between the very general roles and the information contributed by individual lexical verbs to the meaning of a clause. An Agent may be involved in many kinds of action, and a Patient may be unaffected by an action, say *watch*, or be affected to a large extent, as in the actions denoted by *break* or *lift*. Patients can be created, as in *write a book*, or destroyed, as in *burn the manuscript*. Roles do not connect up directly with the world but with the ways in which the speakers of languages conceive of and present situations in the world.

Exercises

1. Examples (34a, b) above demonstrated the difference in meaning between planting a garden with roses and planting roses in a garden. Read the discussion of those examples and consider the examples below. Do they signal the same differences of meaning? Are there examples where the differences in meaning are cancelled by the entities in the situation or by the type of action?

1. The workmen loaded the bricks onto the lorry.
2. The workmen loaded the lorry with the bricks.
3. The vandals sprayed slogans on the wall.
4. The vandals sprayed the wall with slogans.
5. The mechanic sprayed the points with damp start.
6. The mechanic sprayed damp start on the points.
7. The director hung pictures on the walls.
8. The director hung the walls with pictures.
9. Italians supply ice-cream to Scots.
10. Italians supply Scots with ice-cream.
11. Alice crammed the papers into the drawer.
12. Alice crammed the drawer with papers.
13. The author inscribed his signature on the book.
14. The author inscribed the book with his signature.

15. The deer stripped the bark off the tree.
16. The deer stripped the tree of its bark.

2. Which of the following examples do you find acceptable? (In speech, in writing?) The examples in Exercise 1 have the 'same' lexical verb in two different syntactic constructions. Are the following examples similar?

1. Claudia poured water into the bath.
2. Claudia poured the bath with water.
3. Claudia filled water into the bath.
4. Claudia filled the bath with water.
5. The gang stole a million pounds from the bank.
6. The gang stole the bank of a million pounds.
7. The gang robbed a million pounds from the bank.
8. The gang robbed the bank of a million pounds.

3. Assign roles to the nouns in the following extract adapted from William Dalrymple, *From the Holy Mountain*.

I recorded several versions of this story in Urfa (Edessa). Father Abraham was born in a cave on the citadel mount, where he lay hidden from its castellan, Nimrod the Hunter. Nimrod nevertheless tracked down Abraham's cradle and used two pagan pillars on the acropolis as a catapult to propel the baby into a furnace at the bottom of the hill. The Almighty realised that his divine plan for Mankind was in danger, intervened and turned the furnace into a pool full of carp. The carp caught the baby and carried him to the poolside. Abraham promised that anyone who ate the carp would go blind.

12 Grammar and semantics: case, gender, mood

12.1 Introduction

Syntax is of interest (as is morphology too) because without syntax human beings would be unable to construct complex messages conveying information about complex situations, proposals or ideas. We touched on the relationship between grammar and semantics in Chapter 4 on word classes; it turned out that the differences between the major classes of words are central to the use of language. It was not so much the contrast between reference to people, places and things and reference to actions and states as the acts that speakers carry out with different classes of words – referring, predicating and modifying.

One set of criteria for recognising word classes has to do with morphosyntactic properties; in many languages, nouns have suffixes that signal case, while verbs have suffixes that signal person and number (as described in Chapter 5 on the lexicon and in Chapter 9 on syntactic linkage). In many languages, verbs also have suffixes that signal other information that is semantically central. The verb suffixes of Latin, for example, carry information about tense, aspect, mood and voice, 'grammatical categories' which we are about to introduce.

As we saw when we explored word classes in Chapter 4, many languages have a much richer system of noun and verb suffixes (inflectional morphology) than English, whose inflectional morphology is pretty sparse. Much of the work that is done by suffixes in Latin, say, is done by syntactic constructions in English and falls into the scope of this book on two counts, being syntactic and being central to the connections between grammar and meaning.

12.2 Case

We have already discussed the category of case in various places, particularly in Chapter 9 on syntactic linkage where we looked at certain key facts of case in Latin, but also in Chapter 8 on grammatical functions and Chapter 11 on roles. The term 'case' was traditionally used for the system of noun suffixes typical of Indo-European languages. For convenience, we reproduce as (1a) and (1b) below some of the Latin examples discussed in Chapter 9.

(1) a. Latin

    reks gladium ponit
    king sword put-down   'the king put down the sword'

Gladium has the accusative suffix (see Chapter 9 for explanations of the case terms 'accusative', 'nominative' and 'ablative'). Any adjective modifying *gladium* also has to be in the accusative case, as in (1b).

(1) b. reks magnum gladium ponit
    king big sword put-down
    'the king put down the big sword'

(2) a. Latin

    reks gladio utitur
    king sword is-using   'the/a king is using the/a sword'

In (2), *gladio* has the ablative suffix *-o*. Any adjective modifying *gladio* also has to be in the ablative case, as in (2b), where *magno* is the ablative singular form of *magn-*.

(2) b. Latin

    reks magno gladio utitur
    king big sword is-using
    'the/a king is using the/a big sword'

As discussed in Chapter 9, different suffixes are required for plural nouns – *reges* instead of *reks*, *gladiis* instead of *gladio*. Moreover, Latin nouns fall into three major classes and two minor classes, and each class has its own set of case suffixes. The case suffixes signal the relation between the nouns in a clause and the verb, and they signal which adjectives modify which noun and which noun modifies a given preposition (since different prepositions assign different cases). English does not have case suffixes. Pronouns display remnants of the earlier case system – *saw me* vs **saw I*, *to me* vs *to I* – but no case suffixes are added to nouns, and there is no 'agreement' between a noun and the adjectives that modify it.

    English does have the possessive suffix *'s* in *John's bike* and *Juliet's spaniel*. In spoken English, with the exception of irregular nouns such as *children* or *mice*, *'s* is not added to plural nouns. Possession is signalled (in

writing) by an apostrophe added to plural nouns, as in *the dogs' kennel*. The apostrophe has no spoken equivalent. The *'s* suffix is also added to noun phrases rather than nouns, as in *the woman next door's poodle* and *John and Juliet's garden*. An analysis of the possessive suffix goes beyond the scope of this book, but it is clear that it behaves very differently from the case suffixes of languages such as Latin and Russian.

As explained in Chapter 11 on roles, the traditional concept of case has been extended to take in the relationships between verb and nouns in clauses and the ways in which these relationships are signalled. In some languages, the relations are marked by affixes added to the verb, but these would still come under the modern concept of CASE. (It will be helpful to use capital letters when referring to the modern extended concept and small letters when referring to the traditional concept or to affixes or, as in English, to prepositions.) CASE is relevant to English; the relations between verb and nouns in clauses are signalled by position and by the presence or absence of prepositions. In the basic active declarative construction (see Chapter 3), the subject is to the left of the verb, with no preposition, and the direct object is to the right of the verb, with no preposition. In the indirect object construction, the indirect object is immediately to the right of the verb and followed by the direct object. All other nouns in a clause are connected to the verb by a preposition. (Note that this does not mean that all prepositions signal verb–noun relations. They can also signal noun–noun relations, as in *the vase on the table*, and adjective–noun relations, as in *rich in minerals*.) The key question is to what extent any constant meaning attaches to a given preposition wherever it occurs (and, for languages such as Latin and Russian, the extent to which a constant meaning attaches to a given case suffix). This question is discussed in Chapter 11 on roles.

12.3 Gender

In Chapter 9 on syntactic linkage, we mentioned that Latin nouns fall into various classes called 'genders' and that they are misleadingly named 'masculine gender', 'feminine gender' and 'neuter gender'. The different classes of noun are grammatically important because which class a noun belongs to determines which case suffixes it takes and which case suffixes any modifying adjectives take. This is exemplified in (1)–(3) in Chapter 9. English nouns fall into classes that are more closely linked to natural gender. There is a major split between animate and inanimate nouns, linked to the use of *it* as opposed to *he* and *she*. The animate nouns split into male and female, which governs the use of *he* as opposed to *she*.

The labels 'masculine' and so on applied to classes of Latin noun can be seen as not entirely arbitrary if we take into account the fact that nouns denoting women, in whatever capacity, are typically female: *mater* (mother), *filia* (daughter), *femina* (woman) are feminine; *pater* (father), *filius* (son), *vir* (man) are masculine; *servus* is 'male slave', *serva* is 'female slave' and so on. Neuter nouns appear at first sight to offer no generalisation, but an important one can be made: no nouns denoting animate beings are neuter. That generalisation does not apply as neatly to Indo-European languages as a whole, but it remains true that relatively few neuter nouns denote animate beings. The ones that are usually mentioned are the neuter German nouns *Kind* (child), *Weib* (woman), *Mädchen* (girl), *Fräulein* (young woman), *Tier* (animal), *Pferd* (horse), *Krokodil* (crocodile).

Current thinking on gender is that there is always a semantic core to gender systems, but the degree of semantic justification can vary from almost complete to very little. There are languages, such as the Bantu language Luganda, spoken in areas of Uganda and Kenya, which have classes of nouns based on such properties as whether they denote humans, animals, round objects, thin rigid objects, thin flexible objects, and so on. There are many nouns that fit the pattern, but the language has a general class into which go all new or borrowed nouns. Work on the Australian language Dyirbal (North Queensland) has shown that the working of a gender system might require knowledge of a society's myths. In Dyirbal myth, the moon and the sun are husband and wife; the words for moon and husband are together in one class and the words for wife and sun are together in another class. Nouns to do with fire and light go in the same class as the noun for sun. The satin bird brought fire from the clutches of the rainbow snake, and the noun denoting the bird is in the same class as the words for sun and fire. The bite of the hairy mary grub has the same effect as bad sunburn, and the noun denoting that grub is also in the same class as the noun for sun.

12.4 Mood

Throughout this book we have described speakers using syntax in order to talk about situations, adopting different perspectives on a given situation. This was a central part of the discussion of roles in Chapter 11 and continues to be a central part of mood, tense, aspect and voice. It would be very pleasing and appropriate if 'mood' as a technical term in grammar derived from or was historically associated with 'mood' as a term applied to psychological states. Unfortunately it is not, since the latter is cognate with a German word and the former derives from the Latin word which has also survived in Modern English as 'mode'. The

central point is that speakers have different modes of presenting situations.

12.4.1 Statements, questions, commands

1. Speakers can make statements about situations – *This is happening, That happened.*
   They can ask questions about situations and about participants in situations – *Is this happening?, Did that happen?*
   They can require or request that a particular situation be created or not created – *Do this, don't do that.*
2. They can present situations as factual – *This happened, This did happen.*
   They can present situations as possible – *This might happen.*
   They can present situations as necessary – *This has to happen, That must happen.*
3. They can state their authority for making a statement – *Evidently, she has decided to change jobs, I know for a fact that this plane is unsafe.*
4. They can present situations as the objects of wishes, hopes, fears – *I wish he had better manners, She's afraid he's going to make a fool of himself.*

In Chapter 3 on constructions we looked at two of the constructions in (1), the declarative construction and the yes–no interrogative construction. There we described the arrangements of words into phrases and the syntactic differences between the two; here we are interested in the uses to which speakers put the constructions, and add the imperative construction which can be used to issue instructions and requests. (But in many situations, speakers do not use the imperative; see the exercises at the end of the chapter.)

The examples in (3) are not normally discussed under the heading of mood, but the concept of mood should be extended to take them in. One reason is that the distinction between making a statement, asking a question and issuing a command is not sufficient, because speakers make assertions with different degrees of certainty and authority. In English, these degrees are signalled by means of adverbs such as *evidently* or *apparently*, and by phrases such as *for a fact*. There is some controversy as to whether a given speaker makes a stronger assertion by means of *That's the guy who attacked the policemen* or *That must be the guy who attacked the policemen*. An earlier view was that the former was the stronger assertion, but another, more recent, view is that the former is neutral and that it is the speaker who utters *must be* who expresses the stronger commitment to the proposition [THAT GUY ATTACK THE POLICEMEN].

A second reason for extending the discussion is that there are languages, such as Turkish, in which degrees of certainty are obligatorily expressed; speakers who have seen an event with their own eyes must use one set of verb forms while speakers who have not witnessed it but merely heard about it from others must use another set of verb forms.

12.4.2 Subjunctive mood

Any general investigation of mood must deal with the business of speakers making assertions with different degrees of certainty or authority, but the topic is not of central concern here. We are going to focus on (4) and (2) above. The examples in (4) relate to what is called the subjunctive mood. It is unfortunate that 'mood' is applied to this concept, although it is a very old usage and difficult to change. It also has some justification because it is connected with the mode in which speakers choose to present a situation. The term 'subjunctive mood' relates to special sets of verb forms. English used to have such forms; indeed, in a sense it still does have them, but they have fallen into disuse and are now almost archaic. They occur in examples such as *If I were in such difficulties, I would take to my bed*, where *were* occurs with the singular subject. Most speakers and writers nowadays use *was*. Another example, even more unusual, is *be* in *If this be true, the plan should be abandoned*.

The subjunctive forms were used in order to present a situation as remote from reality – the speaker being in difficulties – or as possibly remote from reality – this being true. The technical term is 'non-factual'. Why the mysterious term 'subjunctive'? The examples just given involve subjunctive forms in subordinate clauses – *if I were in such difficulties* and *if this be true*. Subordinate clauses were said to be 'subjoined' to the main clause in a sentence, or to be 'subjuncts'. Hence 'subjunctive'. This brings us back to (4.) and the presentation of situations as the objects of hopes, fears and wishes. To present a situation thus, speakers have to construct a main clause containing a verb such as *hope* or *wish* with a subordinate complement clause expressing the hoped-for situation. This type of construction has disappeared from English but is found in French, as shown in (3).

(3) French

   a. Sa   fille   est première en tout
      His daughter   is   first   in   everything

   b. Il veut que sa fille   soit première en tout
      He wants that his daughter is   first   in everything

The relevant contrast is between *est* (is) in (3a) and *soit* (is) in (3b). In the latter, the speaker states that someone has a wish – *il veut* (he wants) – and states the content of the wish by means of the complement clause *que sa fille soit première en tout* (that his daughter is first in everything). The wished-for situation does not exist at the moment, and this is signalled both by the verb *veut* and by the subjunctive mood. *Est* in (3a) is said to be in the indicative mood. The speaker indicates or refers to a situation which does exist.

12.4.3 Epistemic and deontic modality

The presentation of situations as possible or necessary, point (2.) above, is achieved in English by modal verbs. The essential distinction in this area is between epistemic and deontic modality.

'Epistemic' derives from the Greek *episteme* (knowledge), and epistemic modality relates to the way (the mode) in which speakers know a situation; do they know that it exists, do they consider it as merely possible or do they treat it as necessarily existing (although they have not seen it themselves) on the basis of evidence?

'Deontic' derives from the Greek verb *deo* (tie). Deontic modality relates to whether speakers present a situation as possible because permission has been given, or as necessary because circumstances require it, for example because someone with authority has issued a command or because the situation is such that other actions are ruled out.

Epistemic possibility is expressed by *could, may* or *might,* as in (4).

(4) She could/might/may be in the library (= It is possible that she is in the library)

May is neutral but *might* and *could* express more remote possibility. Note that *can* is not excluded in principle from expressing epistemic possibility but occurs very rarely with this interpretation. In addition to asserting that propositions are epistemically possible, speakers assert that they are epistemically not possible, as in (5).

(5) She may/might not be in her room just now (= It is possible that she is not in her room)

Can/could and *may/might* derive historically from different verbs and diverge in meaning to the extent that *can* and *could* can be used to refer to physical or mental ability, whereas *may* and *might* cannot. Example (6a) is quite different in meaning from (6b).

(6) a. Margaret can/could multiply large numbers in her head (= is/ was able to)
     b. Margaret may/might multiply large numbers in her head (= it

is possible that Margaret will multiply large numbers in her head if you ask her nicely)

When negated, *can* and *could* behave very differently from *may* and *might*. Example (7) expresses a stronger commitment to the impossibility of a situation. The gloss is 'it is not possible that such and such', as opposed to 'it is possible that not such and such' for (5).

(7) She can't be in her room just now. (= It is not possible that she is in her room just now.)

Speakers may also present situations as epistemically necessary, that is, they can convey the message 'I conclude from the evidence that this event happened/is going to happen'. *Must* is typically used, as in (8).

(8) That must be the worst joke I've ever heard.

Speakers also use *have to* and *have got to*, which express necessity but are not modal verbs because they do not have the typical syntax of modal verbs: *That's got to be the worst joke I've ever heard.*

Many examples of epistemic necessity can be glossed by means of *I conclude that*, as in (9), which could be uttered as the speaker looks at piles of empty beer cans.

(9) You must spend a lot of money on beer. [= I conclude that you spend ...]

Speakers can also conclude that something is necessarily not the case. *They can't be going to tell us* used to be the standard British English construction, but *They mustn't be going to tell us* is the regular construction for speakers of Scottish English and speakers of American English and is moving into standard English English.

Deontic possibility has to do with giving or withholding permission. Grammar books used to assert that *may* is used in this sense, but the bulk of speakers both in the UK and in North America use *can*. Permission can be given to do something or not to do something; the latter is typically expressed by verbs other than *may*. Having permission not to do something is equivalent to not being obliged to do something, and the typical expressions are, for example, *You don't have to come to work tomorrow* and *You don't need to come to work tomorrow*. In contrast, not having permission to do something is expressed by *may not* [the standard story] or *can't/cannot*: *You may not/can't/cannot hand in your dissertation late.*

Deontic necessity is expressed by *must*, *have to* and *have got to*. The typical account in grammars of English is that *must* expresses an obligation placed on individuals by themselves (*I must read that new novel because I*

13 Grammar and semantics: aspect, tense, voice

13.1 Aspect

Speakers of any language convey a large amount of information about situations and time. They can represent a given action as ongoing or as completed; they can represent it as having taken place once or as being repeated or as being a habit. We can locate a situation in past, present or future time and we can locate situations in time relative to other situations in a fairly subtle fashion. Whether a situation is ongoing or completed, repeated or habitual comes under the heading of aspect, which can be thought of as the aspect or view which a speaker offers of a particular situation. The location of a situation in past, present or future time, or of two situations relative to each other in time, comes under the heading of tense, which derives from the French word *temps* (time).

13.1.1 *Stative and dynamic verbs and clauses*

In Chapter 5 on the lexicon, we established a connection between specific lexical items and particular constructions. A similar connection exists between specific lexical verbs and aspect, and we begin by looking at the relevant classes of verbs. Analysts distinguish between lexical aspect, the different lexical classes of verbs, and grammatical aspect, the information encoded in the grammars of languages. It is unfortunate that 'aspect' has become ambiguous, but the usage is probably here to stay. An alternative would be to employ the German term 'Aktionsart' (action type) for the lexical classes, as is the practice in work on Slavic languages, and to confine 'aspect' to grammar.

The major distinction splitting verbs into two major lexical classes is between stative and non-stative (or dynamic) verbs. Stative verbs are not difficult to recognise. Consider the examples in (1).

(1) a. What happened?   They went home.
    b. What happened?   *They knew his parents.
    c. What happened?   *They were very cold.

143

If a clause can be used to answer the question *What happened?*, it contains a non-stative (dynamic) verb. If a clause cannot be so used, it contains a stative verb. The second clause in (1a) contains *went*, which is dynamic and relates to an action. *Knew* in (1b) and *were* in (1c) both relate to states and are not dynamic but stative. Stative verbs exclude adverbs such as *quickly*; *They quickly knew his parents* is not acceptable and *They were quickly very cold* is only acceptable if the interpretation is 'they quickly became cold'.

Stative verbs occur either not at all in the Progressive (to be discussed below) or only occasionally. Example (2) is unacceptable, and (3a, b), actual examples uttered by native speakers of English, are very rare.

(2) *We are knowing this theory.
(3) a. They're believing everything you say. [RARE]
     b. You'll soon be owning all the land round here. [RARE]

Stative verbs do not occur in the WH cleft construction. This consists of, for example, *What she did was* followed by a clause. Example (4) is acceptable while (5a, b) are not.

(4) What she did was e-mail all her friends.
(5) a. *What she did was know this theory.
     b. *What she did was be very cold.
     c. *What she did was own all the land round here.

From the above, it is clear that whether a particular lexical verb takes the Progressive or not is a weakish criterion for stative verbs, but that occurrence in the WH cleft construction and occurrence in clauses answering the question *What happened?* are reliable criteria.

13.1.2 Activities, achievements and accomplishments

It is now accepted practice to divide dynamic verbs into three classes. In fact, although people still talk of classes of verbs, it is clear that the relevant distinctions actually hold between whole clauses, so that strictly speaking it is not the verb but the verb plus its complements that is involved. To talk of classes of verbs is not without justification, however; as shown in Chapter 5 on the lexicon and in Chapter 10 on heads, verb phrases and clauses, verbs can be regarded as the heads of clauses and as controlling the types of structures allowed in particular clauses. In many languages, the different clause structures are signalled by differences in the shape of the verb. The three classes of dynamic verbs divide into two groups. The first is that of activity verbs, which denote situations that are seen as going on in the same kind of way over a period of time and

as having no built-in boundary; they allow phrases such as *for hours*. Examples are in (6) and should be contrasted with (7).

(6) a. Harriet talked to Emma for hours.
    b. The dog chased the cat for days.
(7) a. Harriet told Emma the whole story.
    b. The dog caught the cat.

What do we mean by 'built-in boundary'? We are not concerned with the fact that there are natural limitations on activities, that human beings run out of energy and concentration and become hungry and thirsty. The important point is that in the situation described by (7a) the event of telling a story comes to an end when the end of the story is reached. Harriet and Emma can go off to practise their drawing or Emma can tell the story again, but both count as new events. The situation described by (6a) has no built-in boundary; there is no point at which the event of talking comes to an end and a new event starts. The talking presumably ends when Harriet or Emma has had enough or they are interrupted, but the clause tells us nothing about that.

Similarly, the event described by (7b) comes to an end when the dog has trapped the cat; the event described by (6b) has no built-in boundary. The difference is brought out by the kinds of adverbs that can be added; (6a, b) allow adverbs such as *for hours* that accord with an activity being stretched out over time. They exclude adverbs such as *in twenty minutes* which relate to an event reaching its final boundary and being completed. In contrast, (7a, b) allow adverbs such as *in twenty minutes* but exclude adverbs such as *for hours* – *Harriet told Emma the whole story in twenty minutes* is fine, but the following examples are peculiar: **Harriet told Emma the whole story for twenty minutes* and **Harriet talked to Emma in twenty minutes*.

Example (7b) is an instance of an achievement verb. Achievements often have to do with the beginning or end of an event and are conceived of as having no duration. They might be described as being all boundary. Other achievement verbs are *wink, knock, stab*, as in *Mrs Jennings winked at Eleanor*.

The other class of verbs that have a built-in boundary are called accomplishments. They related to situations with two components, an activity phase and then a closing phase. Examples of accomplishment verbs/clauses are given in (8).

(8) a. The beaver built a dam.
    b. Anne played the tune on the piano.

In the situations described by (8a, b), there is an activity phase in which the beaver collects materials, say, and builds the dam higher and higher, and an activity phase in which Anne plays the main body of the tune. These events are brought to a close by the beaver putting the final log or branch in place and Anne playing the final note. One difference between accomplishment and achievement verbs is worth pointing out. Both types can occur in the Progressive, but with different interpretations. *The beaver was building the dam* presents one event of building as ongoing; *Mrs Jennings was winking at Eleanor* is most straightforwardly taken as presenting not one event of winking but several events.

We can summarise the above discussion in the following paragraph and in Table 13.1. Stative verbs do not denote events. They denote states, which do not develop over time in different phases the way that events evolve but remain the same. In English, stative verbs are excluded from clauses answering the question *What happened?*, are excluded from WH clefts and occur rarely in the Progressive. Activity, accomplishment and achievement verbs all denote events. Activities denote events with no built-in boundary and stretching out over time. Achievements denote events conceived of as occupying no time at all. Accomplishments denote events with an activity phase and a closure phase; they can be spread out over time, but there is a built-in boundary. These differences in meaning are reflected in the different sorts of time adverb that can modify the different classes of verb and in the different interpretation of accomplishment and achievement verbs in the Progressive.

Table 13.1

	denotes an event	*conceived as stretching over time*	*has built-in boundary*	*occurs freely in the Progressive*
Stative	no	yes	no	no
Activity	yes	yes	no	yes
Accomplishment	yes	yes	yes	yes
Achievement	yes	no	yes	no

13.1.3 Grammatical aspect in English: Progressive and Simple aspect

Putting stative verbs on one side, we can say that English verbs occur in the Progressive or Simple forms. The Progressive is a syntactic construction consisting of *be* plus the participle in *-ing*. The Simple form consists of just the verb stem plus the suffixes whose central or prototypical forms are *-s* or *-ed*. Examples are given in (9)–(11).

(9) a. Jane was playing the piano.   ACTIVITY
      b. Jane played the piano.
(10) a. Tess was knocking at the door.   ACHIEVEMENT
      b. Tess knocked at the door.
(11) a. Frank Churchill was crossing the street.

                           ACCOMPLISHMENT
      b. Frank Churchill crossed the street.

All the above examples present events as taking place in past time. (Tense and time will be discussed below.) Presented with such examples out of context, native speakers of English take the Progressive examples of ACTIVITY or ACCOMPLISHMENT verbs to present a single event as ongoing. They take the examples with the Simple form as presenting a single completed event. This is not the only possible interpretation of the Simple form in the past tense, for adverbs such as *every day* or *four or five times a day* can be added to examples such as (9b), (10b) and (11b), giving them a habitual interpretation. That is, they present an event as happening regularly over a long period of time, as a habit. Consider now the examples in (12)–(14).

(12) a. Jane is visiting Emma.   ACTIVITY
      b. Jane visits Emma.
(13) a. Tess is knocking at the door.   ACHIEVEMENT
      b. Tess knocks at the door.
(14) a. Frank Churchill is crossing the street. ACCOMPLISHMENT
      b. Frank Churchill crosses the street.

The examples with the Progressive forms, like the ones in (9)–(11), are interpreted as presenting a single event as ongoing. (In the case of the achievement verb in (13), the knocks are repeated, but it is possible to interpret the series of repeated knocks as a single event. For present purposes, we concentrate on (12) and (14).)

Out of context, the Simple forms are typically interpreted as presenting an event as habitual: *Jane visits Emma every Tuesday, Tess always knocks at the door before she comes in, Frank Churchill crosses the street every time he sees Mr Knightley approaching*. These Simple forms in the present tense can be given single-event interpretations, but only in special contexts. One is the 'sporting commentary', with many examples such as *Savage runs up, bowls and Dither is out lbw.* The other is a type of narrative in the present tense, either literary – *Tess knocks at the door. Receiving no reply, she opens it, shouts 'Hello' and goes into the hall* – or joke – *This man goes into a Glasgow bar with a crocodile on a lead and asks the barman 'Do you serve X?'*

Progressive contrasts with Simple, but what exactly is signalled by the contrast? It seems that verbs in the Progressive, whether in past or present tense, are typically used to present a single event as ongoing. The Simple form presents an event as completed. Past-tense Simple forms typically present a single event as completed (but this interpretation can be overruled by an adverb such as *every Friday*). In the present tense, outside the special contexts mentioned above, they are typically interpreted as presenting an event as habitual. That is, verbs in the Simple form present an event as completed but leave it unspecified whether the event is single or repeated. In the past tense, the single-event interpretation is the favourite and neutral, but in present tense the habitual interpretation is the favourite and neutral.

13.2 Tense in English

Traditional grammars of English talk of past, present and future tense. One view is that past and present tense go together, since they are both formed from verb stems plus the suffixes -*s* and -*ed*. (We ignore irregular verbs such as *swim* and the suffix-less present-tense forms.) The traditional future tense is formed from the auxiliary verbs *shall* and *will* plus the verb stem (although many speakers do not use *shall*). That is, the traditional future tense is a syntactic construction but the past and present tenses are single words. This grammatical difference should make us suspect that the 'future tense' is not a tense at all but has some other meaning.

It turns out that the *will* construction does not just place an event in future time but in many cases signals the intention of the speaker; *will* derives historically from a verb that was equivalent to *want* or *intend* and can still be used with this meaning. In examples with first-person subjects, such as *I'll return the book tomorrow* and *I'll meet you at the airport*, the speaker's intention is part of the message. In examples with third-person animate subjects, such as *She'll be in London tomorrow* or *He'll hand in the essay on Friday*, the speaker may be talking about the third person's intentions but may just be making a prediction about a future event. In examples with third-person inanimate subjects, it is difficult to find a reference to intentions; *The snow will arrive tomorrow* is simply a prediction.

The complex interpretation of the 'future tense' construction is not unique to English. In many Indo-European languages, speakers and writers typically refer to future time with verbs of movement. Many instances of a future tense derive historically from verbs of obligation (French) or from verbs of volition (Bulgarian, Modern Greek). Some Native American languages in North America have sets of verb forms that are used for presenting situations as remote from reality (as unreal or irrealis). These forms are also used for referring to situations set in future time.

We talk of future events in terms of intentions and obligations because future time, unlike past and present time, cannot be inspected. Even where verbs of movement are used, as in *I'm going to take the weekend off and start afresh on Monday*, there is a strong element of intention. Where future events are presented by means of present-tense verbs, the events referred to must be part of a schedule or plan that would only fail to operate in most unusual circumstances. Consider (15).

(15) a. Real play Valencia next Sunday.
      b. I leave for Paris next week.

Speakers who utter (15a) or (15b) place the football match and the departure for Paris in present time because the events are known, arranged and regarded as inevitable. They are in the speaker's present time. In contrast, (16) in most contexts is impossible because, outside the world of James Bond films, human beings cannot control volcanoes.

(16) *The volcano erupts on Tuesday.

13.3 The English Perfect

Another syntactic construction central to the tense–aspect system of English is the Perfect, exemplified in (17).

(17) The snow has blocked the track.

Analysts have found it difficult to classify the Perfect as an aspect or a tense. It has two constituents, *has* or *have* and a past participle, here *blocked*. (The label 'participle' is not helpful; it derives from the Latin words meaning 'take part' or 'participate' and is supposed to reflect the fact that in, for example, the Perfect construction, words such as *blocked* participate in two word classes. *Blocked* is related to the verb *block* but is itself a sort of adjective – compare *The blocked track*.) The participle indicates an action that is completed, and this is why the Perfect looks like an aspect; but *has* signals present time, and this makes the Perfect look like a tense. On the assumption that some constructions may simply be indeterminate, we make no attempt here to solve the problem.

The Perfect has been defined as focusing upon the presently accessible consequences of a past event, rather than upon the past event per se; this is summed up in the traditional formula that the Perfect has current relevance. The Perfect in standard written English has four major uses, exemplified in (18).

(18) a. I have written up my thesis. resultative
      b. The Minister has (just) arrived. hot news/recent past
      c. I've been at work for six hours. extended now/persistent situation
      d. Have you ever visited Doubtful Sound?
         Yes, I have been there. experiential/indefinite anterior

Examples (18a–d) go from the most accessible to the least accessible consequences. The speaker who utters (18a) has the finished thesis to show (on disk or in paper form). If (18b) is uttered, the listeners know that the Minister is there with them. The speaker who utters (18c) is saying 'I started work six hours ago and as you can see I am still here, mission unaccomplished'. The consequences of these three examples are visible, as are the consequences of (17), another resultative.

The consequences of (18d) are not so obvious. The question is about a possible visit at an unspecified time in the past, hence the term 'indefinite anterior'. The answer, *Yes, I have been there*, does not specify a time but merely contains an assertion that a visit to Doubtful Sound took place. The consequences might be that the speaker can provide information about how to get to Doubtful Sound, or has happy memories of the landscape and sea, or still has lumps from the bites of the amazingly vicious sandflies.

The English Perfect has been the subject of much debate and analysis, and we can do no more than indicate the main points. We close this section with comments on three aspects of the English Perfect that are in need of investigation. Insufficient attention has been given to the role of *just*, in (18b), and of *ever*, in (18d), as demarcating the hot-news Perfect and the experiential Perfect from the other interpretations. Should (18b) and (18d) be treated as separate constructions, not just separate interpretations?

In written English the Perfect excludes definite time adverbs – *The snow has blocked the track last Monday evening*. This appears to be because the Perfect focuses on the current, accessible consequences of an action, and speakers using the Perfect are not concerned with the action and time of action in the past. In spoken English, particularly spontaneous spoken English, this exclusion of definite past-time adverbs is beginning to break down.

Finally, we should note that past participles were originally resultative, that is, they expressed the result of a completed action. The participles survive in a number of resultative constructions, not just in the resultative Perfect. Examples are given in (19). They are all examples taken from spontaneous speech.

(19) a. You have access to a vein gained and a cardiac analysis done
         within one minute.   [Radio discussion]
      b. That's him consulted.   [TV comedy]
      c. That's you finished.   [task-related dialogue]
      d. There's something fallen down the sink. [conversation]
      e. She needs collected at four o'clock.   [Scottish English
                                         conversation]

13.4 Voice

The category of voice has to do with the different constructions available for taking an event or state and presenting it from different perspectives. (The Latin term from which it derives was used both for voice
in its phonetic sense and for the form of a word. From the latter use came
the third use for active and passive constructions, justified by the fact that
Latin and Greek had different sets of active suffixes and passive suffixes,
as shown in (24a–c).) Suppose we take a situation in which someone
attacked someone else. We can to choose to keep all the participants out
of our report by using (20).

(20) There was an attack yesterday.

13.4.1 The passive

We can choose to mention the person(s) attacked, the Patient(s), but to
leave out the attacker(s). This is done by using the passive construction,
in which the Patient noun, here *Emma and Harriet*, is the subject.

(21) Emma and Harriet were attacked yesterday.

If we want to make sure that our addressee gets all the details, we
mention the Agent and the Patient, and we have a choice of construction,
as in (22).

(22) a. Emma and Harriet were attacked by those ruffians.
      b. Those ruffians attacked Emma and Harriet yesterday.

Example (20) is an instance of what is called the existential construction,
so-called because speakers use it to talk about the existence of people,
things, ideas and whole events. We say nothing more about it here. We
pass on to two of the three major constructions that are our concern.
Consider the passive in (21). This is the main use of the passive both in
speech and in writing: to mention only the Patient and to omit the Agent.
From passives such as (21), listeners can infer an Agent, and adverbs can

be inserted, such as *deliberately* in (23), which bring the Agent very close without actually mentioning who played that role.

(23) The vase was smashed deliberately.

Examples (21) and (23) are instances of the 'short passive', while (22a) is an example of the 'long passive'. Even in the long passive, the Agent noun is in an optional prepositional phrase and is presented as peripheral.

Other languages, such as Latin, also have a construction which allows speakers to omit Agents. The major difference between English and Latin is that Latin verbs take different suffixes in the passive whereas English employs a syntactic construction with an auxiliary verb and a passive participle. A Latin example is given in (24b).

(24) a. servus   regem   occidit
          Slave   king   is-killing
          'A slave is killing the king'

      b. reks   occiditur
          king   is-being-killed
          'The king is being killed'

      c. reks   a   servo   occiditur
          king   from   slave   is-being-killed
          'The king is being killed by a slave'

The case suffixes in Latin have already been discussed in Chapter 9 on syntactic linkage; in fact (24a) is taken from that chapter. The phrase *a servo* in (24c) is a prepositional phrase and optional, as shown by (24b) without it. The passive suffix (third person singular present tense indicative mood) is *-itur* as opposed to *-it* in (24a).

English has another passive construction with the auxiliary verb *get*, as shown in (25).

(25) The sheep got infected with scrapie.

The *get* passive is dynamic. An example such as *The vase was broken* is ambiguous; it can be interpreted either as describing an event in which someone broke the vase or as describing the state in which the vase is – the speaker might point to the bits of the vase lying on a table. *The vase got broken* can only be used to describe an event. This difference comes largely from the fact that *be* is a colourless verb that relates to states and locations and membership of groups (see the different copula constructions described in Chapter 3), while *get* is basically a verb of movement – *We got to Cupar in an hour* – which has been extended to changes in state – *The sky got dark, We got cold.*

There has been some controversy over the *get* passive. Some analysts see a contrast in meaning between (26), with *were*, and (27), with *got*, and treat (28) as unacceptable.

(26) The fans were deliberately provoked by a rival group.
     [The rival group acted deliberately]

(27) The fans got deliberately provoked by a rival group.
     [The fans acted deliberately]

(28) Six students got shot accidentally.

Example (28) is allegedly unacceptable because of a mismatch between the use of *got* and the use of *accidentally*. *Got* can supposedly be used only if the students acted deliberately. There is no support for this analysis in any British corpus. The *get* passive is simply a major passive in spontaneous spoken English. One sample of conversation recorded in Edinburgh had eighteen *be* passives and eleven *get* passives; another had fifty-seven *get* passives and three *be* passives.

Interestingly, examples of *get* passives can be found in written English in which it is quite clear that there is no question of the Patient acting deliberately to cause an action, either because the Patient is inanimate, as in (29), or because the event cannot be controlled by the Patient, as shown by (30).

(29) Some gifts get used a dozen or so times a year.
     [advertisement]

(30) We haven't had a man catch the midday [train] since young Simpkins got sent home with chickenpox last summer.
     [Dick Francis, *Nerve*]

Where speakers do want to indicate that a Patient acted deliberately, they use the reflexive pronoun *himself*, as in (31), from spontaneous conversation.

(31) It's his pal that I mean his pal sort of sits back and eggs him on and of course he gets himself landed into it. [conversation]

We have focused on Agents not being mentioned, but some lexical verbs allow Patients not to be mentioned, as in (32).

(32) a. Can't you see I'm reading?
     b. People go hunting in the Autumn.
     c. We spent yesterday cooking.

The Patients can be omitted in (32) because they are closely connected with the activity denoted by the verb. People read books and news-papers, they hunt foxes, pheasants or deer and they cook food. Patient NPs can also be omitted in clauses describing habitual actions. The best examples relate to tasks or posts within organisations, as in (33a), but any transitive can occur without its Patient NP provided the clause describes a habitual event, as in (33b).

(33) a. She buys for Harrods.
     b. I saw and he chops.

13.4.2 The middle

The third major construction in English is the middle. Typical middles listed in grammars of English are given in (34). They have to do with permanent properties of entities.

(34) a. This sweater washes well.
     b. This book reads well.

Many middles have what is called as 'episodic' interpretation, that is, they denote a single episode or event. Examples are in (35).

(35) a. These cars sold very quickly last week.
     b. It will take years for the Mersey to clean.
     c. The course is jumping well.
     d. One bomb didn't guide and crashed.

Example (35a) refers to a single event of selling; (35b) refers to a single, albeit lengthy, cleaning event; (35c) refers to a property of a particular course at a particular period of time; and (35d) refers to a single event of a bomb failing to guide and crashing.

Some analysts see the middle construction as having a strong re-semblance to the passive, but there is little justification for this view. (The name 'middle', which corresponds to the ancient name given to the equivalent construction in Classical Greek, captures the idea that this construction is neither fully active nor fully passive but in the middle.) The obvious point to make is that English middle clauses and English passive clauses share no syntactic properties; middles can only contain one noun phrase and the verb is active, whereas passives can contain a subject noun phrase and a second noun phrase preceded by *by*, as noted above. The middle construction has no auxiliary verb, whereas the passive has the auxiliary verbs *be* or *get*.

What type of participant is denoted by the subject noun phrase in middle clauses? In passive clauses, the subject noun phrase refers to an entity undergoing some process, that is to a Patient. *The vase was/got broken* and *This candidate was elected* are answers to questions such as *What happened to the vase?* and *What happened to this candidate?* Does the subject noun phrase in a middle clause denote a Patient? The sentence *His novels sell very well* has been said to present the books as 'selling themselves', and this analysis seems to be on the right track. There is no contradiction between two examples referring to the same novel such as *This novel reads very well* and *It is a pity that nobody reads this novel nowadays.* It is quite possible to say *These cars sold very quickly last week* and then add *in spite of the inept performance of our new sales staff.* The expert knitter or tailor who declares *This wool knitted up without any trouble* and *The cloth was cutting beautifully* is not taking credit but giving it to the wool and the cloth.

Example (35b) above was uttered in a television documentary dealing with the River Mersey. The interviewer had been talking to various people about the initial part of the cleaning-up programme, namely the enforcement of legislation to stop factories discharging noxious materials into the river. Thereafter, the river had simply to be left to, as it were, get on with the task of removing the poisons already in the water, and it was in this context that (35b) was uttered.

The person uttering (35d) was attributing blame to the bomb, which refused to respond to the guiding signals and crashed, killing civilians. Example (35c) was uttered by a participant in equestrian cross-country trials, and the burden of the message was that the course permitted accurate jumping of the obstacles and good times for the circuits of the course.

In the light of the above, what role can we assign to the referents of subject noun phrases in middle clauses – Agent or Patient, or some other role? The 'middle' construction is so-called because it is felt to be intermediate between the active and passive constructions Part of the in-between-ness of the construction lies in the question of role, but the problem can be solved if we recognise that, like so many concepts in linguistic analysis, central prototype instances have to be distinguished from peripheral instances. The subject noun phrases in (35a–d) do not refer to prototypical Agents; the referents are not human, do not exercise will-power and do not have goals and intentions. Nonetheless, they are not presented as Patients.

A solution that resolves the contradictions is to regard the subject nouns in the middle construction as Neutral (between Agent and Patient) but as controlling the situations. The cars, by their qualities, determine the rate at which people buy them; the river Mersey, with the powers of cleansing and rejuvenation inherent in clean, flowing water, determines how long it will be before the pollutants are removed altogether; the course, with its fences of a certain height and width, and its obstacles and the state of the ground, determines how successful the horses and riders will be. Finally, the strong impression was given by the spokesman who uttered (35d) that it was the bomb's fault that civilians were killed.

13.5 Conclusion

We have given a brief introduction to case, gender, mood, aspect, tense and voice. For initial elementary discussions, it is convenient to put the six topics into six pigeonholes; but, as with the other concepts in this book, which keep turning up in their own chapter and in other chapters, these six grammatical categories cannot be kept neatly apart. Tense and aspect are closely connected in every language which has both (some languages are reputed to have aspectual distinctions but no tense system), and in English and other languages tense and mood interact. The pairs of sentences in (36)–(37) are distinguished in that the (a) examples have what looks like present tense while the (b) examples have what looks like past tense.

(36) a. Fiona may be here by 5 o'clock.
     b. Fiona might be here by 5 o'clock.
(37) a. If Fiona is here by 5 o'clock, we can go to the party.
     b. If Fiona was/were here by 5 o'clock, we could go to the party.

The past-tense forms do not relate to past time. In their basic uses, present tense relates to present time, which is close to speaker and hearer, and past tense relates to past time, which is more remote from speaker and hearer. In (36b) and (37b), the apparent past-tense forms have nothing to with past time but present a situation as remote from reality. Examples (36a) and (37a) present the situations as much closer to reality. Example (38a) presents the situation of Fiona getting a job as something that should have happened some time ago, that is, the concept of past time is relevant, but also as a situation that is remote from current reality. Note that this construction is only for the presentation of situations as remote; present tense is not possible, as the incorrectness of (38b) shows.

(38) a. It's high time Fiona got a job.
     b. *It's high time Fiona gets a job.

Tense, aspect and mood apart, further investigation of this area of grammar would soon reveal that the old dichotomy of transitive and intransitive (see Chapter 3) is insufficient and has to be replaced by a scale of transitivity in which tense, aspect, mood, case and voice all play a part.

Summary

Aspect and tense have to do with situations and time. Aspect, as in *wrote* vs *was writing*, signals whether an situation is presented as completed or as ongoing, i.e. as having reached its boundary in time or as occupying a period of time. Tense has to do with speakers locating a situation in time – past time as in *She wrote*, present time as in *She is writing* or future time as in *She will write*. One controversy is whether it is legitimate to recognise a future tense. Reference to future time is often achieved by means of a verb such as *will* or *go* combined with another verb, whereas speakers refer to present and past time by means of a single verb. Voice also relates to situations, not to time but to which participants in a situation are presented to the hearer/reader and which participants are presented as central. Speakers use active clauses to present Agents and Patients as central and passive clauses to exclude Agents: *Susan wrote the letter yesterday* vs *The letter was written yesterday*. The middle construction allows speakers to present the non-agent participant as central and as controlling the situation. In *The door won't unlock*, the door is presented as controlling the actions of the other participants by its refusal to unlock. The problem lies not in the clumsiness of the human participant but in some property of the door's lock.

Exercises

1. *The dog was chasing the cat* is a clause denoting an activity. It entails the same clause but with the Simple Past form of the verb, *The dog chased the cat*. That is, whenever the former is true, so is the latter. This entailment does not apply to clauses denoting accomplishments: *Jane was crossing the street* does not entail *Jane crossed the street*. The latter is true only if Jane reached the other side, but the progressive leaves it open whether she did or did not reach the other side: *Jane was crossing the street and in fact reached the other side* vs *Jane was crossing the street when she was run down by a fully laden timber lorry*.

Examine the pairs of clauses below. Which clauses with the verb in the progressive entail the corresponding clause with the verb in the simple past?

1. (a) Harriet was talking to Emma.
   (b) Harriet talked to Emma.

2. (a) The beaver was building a dam.
   (b) The beaver built a dam.
3. (a) Anne Elliott was studying Italian.
   (b) Anne Elliott studied Italian.
4. (a) Mr Knightley was riding to Kingston.
   (b) Mr Knightley rode to Kingston.
5. (a) Mr Knightley was riding towards Kingston.
   (b) Mr Knightley rode towards Kingston.
6. (a) The girls were walking in the gardens.
   (b) The girls walked in the gardens.
7. (a) They were drinking a bottle of Mr Weston's good wine.
   (b) They drank a bottle of Mr Weston's good wine.
8. (a) They were drinking bottles of Mr Weston's good wine.
   (b) They drank bottles of Mr Weston's good wine.

2. Which of the following clauses contain stative verbs? (Apply the tests:
Can they be used to answer the question *What happened?* Can they be
fitted into a WH cleft: *What she did was break the glass with a hammer* vs *What
she did was know all the answers?* The latter is at the very least peculiar.
Does the verb occur easily in the Progressive? *She was writing her report* vs
*She was knowing the details of the case.)

  1. Mr Dashwood died at a very awkward time.
  2. Mrs Dashwood believed that her stepson would be generous.
  3. Eleanor thought that her mother was mistaken.
  4. Eleanor thought about the problem and found a solution.
  5. Mr Woodhouse heard a strange noise.
  6. Mr Woodhouse listened to the strange noise.
  7. Anne understood the words of the Italian songs.
  8. She saw the storm approaching.
  9. She saw how to solve the problem.
 10. She saw (= received) the unexpected guests in the hall.

3. Future time is referred to by *will*, *shall* and *be going to*. Consider the
sentences below. Are any of them unacceptable? Are there differences of
meaning between *be going to* and *will* – that is, are there pairs of examples
that would be used in different circumstances?

  1. (a) She's going to sack all the senior managers (if they don't
         improve their performance).
     (b) She'll sack all the senior managers (if they don't improve their
         performance).
  2. (a) Will I shut the window?

    (b) Am I going to shut the window?

3. (a) Will you shut the window please?
    (b) Shall you shut the window please?
    (c) Are you going to shut the window please?

4. A and B walking to the cinema. A says:
    (a) Hurry up! The film is just going to start.
    (b) Hurry up! The film will just start.

5.   A: where's Fiona?
    (a) B: she'll be in the library I suppose   she had to return some books.
    (b) B: she's going to be in the library I suppose   she had to return some books.

Appendix 1

The examples below – all taken from Chapter 1 – show one notation for marking heads and modifiers. Arrows go from each head to its modifiers.

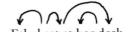

1. Ethel sat at her desk.

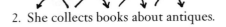

2. She collects books about antiques.

3. We bought some expensive books.

4. My mother bought a present for Jeanie in Jenners last Tuesday.

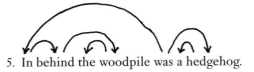

5. In behind the woodpile was a hedgehog.

6. An owl swooped on the rabbit from up in the beech tree.

7 More accountants would make a difference to my income.

8. Would more accountants make a difference to my income?

9. This gritter spread less salt than that one.

Appendix 2

The examples below – all taken or adapted from Chapter 2 – show how diagrams can be used to show the arrangements of words into phrases and phrases into clauses or into bigger phrases. The diagrams are called 'tree diagrams'. This appendix is merely an indication of how they can be used to convey information about the syntactic structure of phrases and clauses. The essential point is that whatever is judged, the best analysis of a given phrase or clause can be shown in a tree diagram.

Consider example 1 below, *the splendid house*. We put a point on the page; the point represents the slot that can be occupied by a noun phrase, and is so labelled. From that point, we draw two lines down to two more points. One point represents the slot that can be occupied by a determiner. The other represents the slot occupied by the remainder of the noun phrase. The reason for this grouping is that, for example, speakers and writers use the determiner *the* to pick out *splendid house* as the thing they wish to draw attention to; not *house* on its own but *splendid house*. The diagrams consist of higher nodes from which lines drop to lower nodes. Some nodes represent slots where sequences of words can occur and are labelled 'noun phrase', 'adjective phrase' and so on. Other nodes represent slots where single words occur and are labelled 'noun', 'preposition' and so on.

In the examples below, their number in Chapter 2 is given in parentheses.

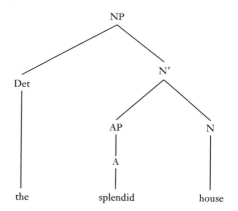

Figure 1 (1b)   the splendid house

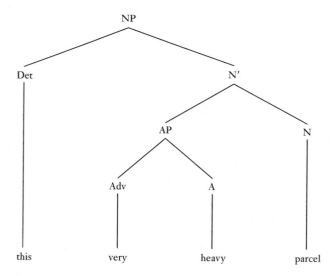

Figure 2 (7)   this very heavy parcel

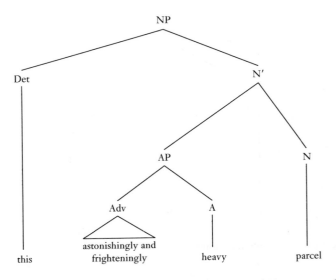

Figure 3 (section 2.2.1)   this astonishingly and frighteningly heavy parcel

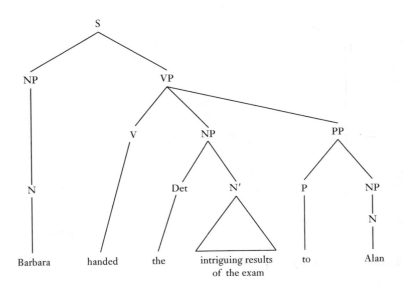

Figure 4 (9a)   Barbara handed the intriguing results of the exam to Alan

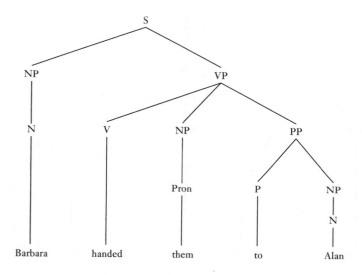

Figure 5 (18)   Barbara handed them to Alan

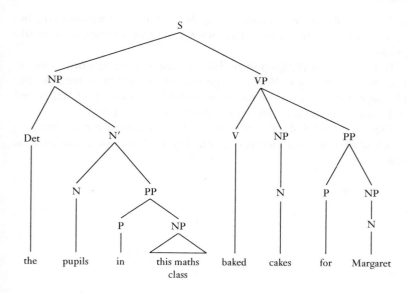

Figure 6 (6a)   The pupils in this maths class baked cakes for Margaret

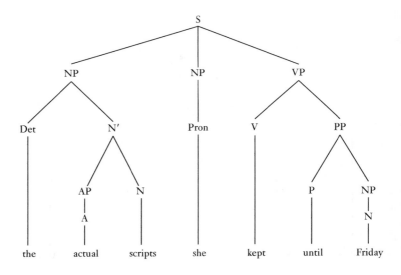

Figure 7 (section 2.2.1)   The actual scripts she kept until Friday

Comments

In Figure 2 above, *very* modifies *heavy*. *Heavy* can occur without *very*, but *very* requires another word. The two fill the slot assigned to adjective phrases.

In Figure 3 above, *heavy* is modified by the conjoined words *astonishingly* and *frighteningly*. We do not go into the structure of the adjective phrase, but inside it is a slot for determiner phrases which is filled by *very* in Figure 2 and by *astonishingly* and *frighteningly* in Figure 3.

Figures 4 and 5 show that *them* can be substituted for *the intriguing results of the exam* and vice versa, and they both occupy a noun-phrase slot.

Appendix 3

Someone is the secretary
[COPULA, DECLARATIVE, ACTIVE]

Angus is the secretary
[COPULA, DECLARATIVE, ACTIVE]

Who is the secretary?
[COPULA, INTERROGATIVE, WH]

Is Angus the secretary?
[COPULA, INTERROGATIVE, YES–NO]

Figure 1

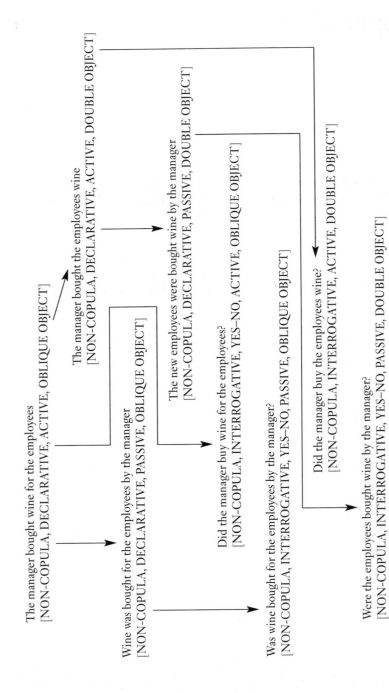

The manager bought wine for the employees
[NON-COPULA, DECLARATIVE, ACTIVE, OBLIQUE OBJECT]

The manager bought the employees wine
[NON-COPULA, DECLARATIVE, ACTIVE, DOUBLE OBJECT]

Wine was bought for the employees by the manager
[NON-COPULA, DECLARATIVE, PASSIVE, OBLIQUE OBJECT]

The new employees were bought wine by the manager
[NON-COPULA, DECLARATIVE, PASSIVE, DOUBLE OBJECT]

Did the manager buy wine for the employees?
[NON-COPULA, INTERROGATIVE, YES–NO, ACTIVE, OBLIQUE OBJECT]

Was wine bought for the employees by the manager?
[NON-COPULA, INTERROGATIVE, YES–NO, PASSIVE, OBLIQUE OBJECT]

Did the manager buy the employees wine?
[NON-COPULA, INTERROGATIVE, ACTIVE, DOUBLE OBJECT]

Were the employees bought wine by the manager?
[NON-COPULA, INTERROGATIVE, YES–NO, PASSIVE, DOUBLE OBJECT]

Figure 2

Discussion of the exercises

Chapter 1

1. 1. *Sir Thomas*: obligatory, complement
      with Edmund: not obligatory, but *agreed* requires *with*. This infor-
      mation goes into the lexical entry for *agree*.
   2. *Mr Elton*: obligatory, complement
      a charade: obligatory, complement
      to Emma: optional but excluded by many verbs and therefore a
      complement
      for a friend: optional, adjunct
   3. *She*: obligatory, complement
      the document: obligatory, complement
      into her briefcase: obligatory, complement
   4. *Raskolnikov*: obligatory, complement
      the old woman: obligatory, complement
      with an axe: optional, adjunct
   5. *Mr D'Arcy*: obligatory, complement
      the Gardiners: obligatory, complement
      at Pemberley: optional, adjunct
      in the summer: optional, adjunct
   6. *Frank*: obligatory, complement
      a piano: obligatory, complement
      to Jane Fairfax: excluded by many verbs, complement
   7. *The porter*: obligatory, complement
      the letter: obligatory, complement
      on the secretary's desk: obligatory, complement
   8. *Harriet*: obligatory, complement
      that Mr Elton would propose to her: obligatory, complement
   9. *The picnic*: obligatory, complement
      at Box Hill: optional, adjunct
      in the summer: optional, adjunct
   10. *He*: obligatory, complement

great vengeance: obligatory, complement
upon them: obligatory, complement
with furious rebukes: optional, adjunct

11. *We*: obligatory, complement
the worst: obligatory, complement
that day in 1968: optional, adjunct

12. *The report*: obligatory, complement
the proposals for the chief executive: obligatory, complement
or
the proposals: obligatory, complement
for the chief executive: optional, adjunct

2. 1. *I*: head (with no modifiers)
ate breakfast in a vast Viennese ballroom with a sprung wooden floor and dadoes dripping with recently reapplied gilt:
ate: head of the above phrase
breakfast: head (with no modifiers)
in: head of the phrase from *in* to *gilt*. Modified by the phrase running from *a vast* to *recently applied gilt*.
ballroom: head of the phrase running from *a vast* to *gilt*. It has four modifiers: *a, vast, Viennese* and the phrase *with a ... applied gilt*.
vast: head with no modifiers (cf. *exceedingly vast*)
Viennese: head with no modifiers (cf. *surprisingly Viennese*)
with: head of and modified by the phrase running from *a sprung* to *applied gilt*
floor: head of the phrase from *a sprung* to *floor* and modified by three modifiers: *a, sprung* and *wooden*
dadoes: head of the phrase running from *dadoes* to *gilt* and modified by the phrase from *dripping* to *gilt*
dripping: head of the phrase from *dripping* to *gilt* and modified by *with recently applied gilt*
with: head modified by *recently applied gilt*
gilt: head modified by *recently applied*
applied: head modified by *recently*

2. *lift*: head modified by *the*
is: head of phrase from *is* to *palms*, modified by the phrase from *a* to *palms*
birdcage: head modified by four modifiers: *a, giant, baroque, entered through a rainforest of potted palms*
giant: head with no modifiers
baroque: head with no modifiers (cf. *thrillingly baroque*)
entered: head modified by the phrase *through ... palms*

through: head modified by *a rainforest of potted palms*
rainforest: head modified by two modifiers: *a* and *of potted palms*
of: head modified by *potted palms*
palms: head modified by *potted*
potted: head with no modifiers (cf. *expertly potted*)

3. *On*: head modified by *the wall.*
   (*Nearby* could be analysed as modifying *wall* or as an independent
   adverbial phrase. In either analysis, it is a head with no modifier:
   cf. *very nearby.*)

wall: head modified by *the* and *newly dusted*
dusted: head modified by *newly*
is: head modified by the phrase *a framed ... Ham*
diploma: head modified by *a*, *framed*, the phrase *from ... Exhibition*
   and the phrase *signed ... Ham*
framed: head with no modifiers (cf. *elegantly framed*)
from: head modified by *the 1932 ... Exhibition*
Exhibition: head modified by *the*, *1932*, and *Ideal Homes*
Homes: head modified by *Ideal*
Ideal: head with no modifiers (cf. *Completely Ideal*)
signed: head modified by *by the mayor of East Ham*
by: head modified by *the mayor of East Ham*
mayor: head modified by *the* and *of East Ham*
of: head modified by *East Ham*
Ham: head modified by *East*
East: head with no modifier

Chapter 2

1. 2. *There* is substituted for *in the drawer.*
   3. *Into the top drawer of the bureau* is transposed, occurring in a different
      slot in a different construction in (3).
   4. *Into the top drawer of the bureau* is transposed into a different slot in
      the same construction as in (1).
   5. *Into the top drawer of the bureau* is transposed into a different slot in a
      different construction from the one in (1).
   6. *Into the top drawer of the bureau* is coordinated with the single word
      there.
   7. *Into the top drawer of the bureau* is transposed into a different slot in
      the same construction as in (1).

2. 1. *The pedestrians offended by the dangerously selfish action of the driver*:
      Noun Phrase

offended by the dangerously selfish action of the driver: Participle Phrase
(*offended* is a Participle)
by the dangerously selfish action of the driver: Prepositional Phrase
the dangerously selfish action of the driver: Noun Phrase
dangerously selfish: Adjective Phrase
of the driver: Prepositional Phrase
the driver: Noun Phrase
threatened to throw him into the harbour: Verb Phrase
to throw him into the harbour: Infinitive Phrase
him: Noun Phrase
into the harbour: Prepositional Phrase
the harbour: Noun Phrase

2. *To throw him into the harbour*: Infinitive Phrase
him: Noun Phrase
into the harbour: Prepositional Phrase
the harbour: Noun Phrase
was illegal but an understandable reaction by the visitors on the quayside: Verb Phrase
illegal: Adjective Phrase
an understandable reaction by the visitors on the quayside: Noun Phrase
understandable: Adjective Phrase
by the visitors on the quayside: Prepositional Phrase
the visitors on the quayside: Noun Phrase
on the quayside: Prepositional Phrase
the quayside: Noun Phrase

3. *Brazil's tropical forests*: Noun Phrase
tropical: Adjective Phrase
Brazil's: Noun Phrase (possessive)
are amazingly rich in fauna and flora: Verb Phrase
amazingly rich in fauna and flora: Adjective Phrase
in fauna and flora: Prepositional Phrase
fauna and flora: Noun Phrase (consisting of two conjoined Noun Phrases, *fauna* and *flora*)

4. *The person sitting at the window*: Noun Phrase
sitting at the window: Participle Phrase (*sitting* is a Participle)
at the window: Prepositional Phrase
the window: Noun Phrase
is my wife: Verb Phrase
my wife: Noun Phrase

5. *Sitting at the window*: free Participle Phrase
at the window: Prepositional Phrase
the window: Noun Phrase

my wife: Noun Phrase
noticed our neighbour's dog: Verb Phrase
our neighbour's dog: Noun Phrase
6. *Susan*: Noun Phrase
   always drinks black coffee: Verb Phrase
   black coffee: Noun Phrase
   black: Adjective Phrase
7. *Susan*: Noun Phrase
   always drinks her coffee black: Verb Phrase
   her coffee: Noun Phrase
   black: Adjective Phrase
8. *In his usual carefree fashion*: Prepositional Phrase
   his usual carefree fashion: Noun Phrase
   usual: Adjective Phrase
   carefree: Adjective Phrase
   John: Noun Phrase
   ran up an enormous bill: Verb Phrase
   an enormous bill: Noun Phrase
   enormous: Adjective Phrase
9. *In his exuberance*: Prepositional Phrase
   his exuberance: Noun Phrase
   John: Noun Phrase
   ran up an enormous hill: Verb Phrase
   up an enormous hill: Prepositional Phrase
   an enormous hill: Noun Phrase
   enormous: Adjective Phrase

Chapter 3

1. 1. Colonel Brandon read poems to Marianne.
       [NON-COPULA, DECLARATIVE, ACTIVE, OBLIQUE OBJECT]
    2. Mrs Gardiner was Mrs Bennet's sister.
       [COPULA, DECLARATIVE, EQUATIVE]
    3. Who was Jane Bennett's suitor?
       [COPULA, INTERROGATIVE, WH, EQUATIVE]
    4. Why did Frank Churchill deceive everybody?
       [NON-COPULA, INTERROGATIVE, WH, ACTIVE]
    5. When was Emma scolded by Mr Knightley?
       [NON-COPULA, INTERROGATIVE, WH, ACTIVE, OBLIQUE OBJECT]

6. Was Mr Knightley much older than Emma?
   [COPULA, INTERROGATIVE, YES–NO, ASCRIPTIVE]
7. Where did Captain Wentworth propose to Anne Elliott?
   [NON-COPULA, INTERROGATIVE, WH, ACTIVE, OBLIQUE OBJECT]
8. Sir Walter Elliott was in Bath.
   [COPULA, DECLARATIVE, LOCATIVE]
9. Did Colonel Brandon bring Marianne books?
   [NON-COPULA, INTERROGATIVE, YES–NO, DOUBLE OBJECT]
10. Elizabeth Bennett was at first unimpressed with Mr D'Arcy.
    [COPULA, DECLARATIVE, ASCRIPTIVE]

2. 1. [COPULA, DECLARATIVE, LOCATIVE]
      We were in London.
   2. [NON-COPULA, DECLARATIVE, PASSIVE]
      Our luggage was sent to Berlin.
   3. [NON-COPULA, INTERROGATIVE, YES–NO, DOUBLE OBJECT]
      Did you tell Lydia the news?
   4. [COPULA, INTERROGATIVE, YES–NO, ASCRIPTIVE]
      Is Fiona really ill?
   5. [NON-COPULA, INTERROGATIVE, WH, PASSIVE]
      Why was our luggage sent to Berlin?
   6. [COPULA, INTERROGATIVE, WH, EQUATIVE]
      Who was the Prime Minister at that time?

Chapter 4

1. Adjectives:
   Decrepit Victorian sporadic steep still fragrant highest gentle
   Verbs:
   covered pirouetted skating emerged slid opened befell

2. MEET
   1. Sue met Lionel at the conference.
   2. Sue and Lionel met at the conference.
   3. Sue met Lionel at the airport (and drove him home).
   4. *Sue and Lionel met at the airport.
      (with the interpretation 'Sue went to the airport to meet Lionel')
   5. Sue met with Lionel at the café.
   Note: *Sue met at the conference.
         (5) is not acceptable to all speakers of English.

SCATTER
  6. The bricks scattered over the floor.
  7. The sugar scattered over the floor.
  8. The baby scattered the bricks over the floor.
  9. The girl scattered the sugar over the floor.
 10. The crowd scattered when the firing began.
Note: *The girl scattered the brick over the floor.
         *The brick scattered over the floor.

COLLIDE
 11. The car and the bus collided.
 12. The car collided with the bus.
Question: Do (11) and (12) have the same meaning?
Note: *The car collided.

CRASH
 13. The car crashed.
 14. The car crashed into the wall.
 15. The car and the bus crashed.
 16. The car and the bus crashed into each other.
 17. The young driver crashed his car.
Question: Do (15) and (16) have the same meaning?

MIX
 18. Dan mixed the ingredients.
 19. Dan mixed the flour into the milk.
 20. Dan mixed the flour with the milk.
 21. Dan mixed with the guests.
 22. Dan mixed a drink.
 23. The ingredients didn't mix.

BLEND
 24. The machine blended the ingredients instantly.
 25. The ingredients blended perfectly.
 26. Blend the carrots with the turnip.

STIR
 27. Mary stirred the soup.
 28. Mary stirred the vegetables into the stock.
 29. The dog stirred when the doorbell rang.

3. RICH meets all the criteria. AWAKE meets one criterion; it occurs after
the verb *be*. MAJOR does not take *-er* or *-est* and does not combine with
more or *most*. WOODEN does not take *-er* or *-est* and does not combine
with *more* or *most* in its literal meaning. When it is applied, for

example, to someone's expression or acting, it does combine with *more* and *most*: *This is the most wooden acting I've ever seen.*

Chapter 5

1. BECOME: copula
   ANTAGONISE: transitive
   FIND: transitive
   HANG: transitive locative (*hung the picture on the wall*)
         intransitive locative (*the picture was hanging on the office wall*)
         transitive (*We'll hang the pictures tomorrow*)
   SUSPEND: transitive locative (*suspended the chandelier from the roof*)
   SEND: ditransitive, transitive directional
   LOCK: transitive, intransitive (*This door locks easily*)
   TURN: intransitive (*The dog turned and barked*)
         transitive (*Turn the page now*)
         copula (*She turned pale*)

2. Modal verbs combine directly with *not* – as in (2); ordinary verbs require the support of *do*, as in (4).
   Modal verbs are placed at the front of interrogative clauses, as in (5); ordinary verbs require the support of *do*, as in (6).
   Modal verbs occur in questions tagged onto declarative clauses, as in (7); ordinary verbs require the support of *do*, as in (8).
   Modal verbs can carry emphasis, as in (9); ordinary verbs require the support of *do*, as in (10).
   Ordinary verbs have forms in *-ing*, as in (11); modal verbs do not.

3. *Ought* is partly like modal verbs in its grammar, as in (1) and (2). However, it requires *to* (*ought to pay attention* vs *must pay attention*) and has the support of *do* in negative clauses and in tag questions, as in (5).
   Need is like a modal verb in combining directly with the negative as in (10) and occurring at the front of interrogative clauses as in (9). It is like ordinary verbs, having an *-ing* form, as in (1), and having the support of *do* in interrogative and negative clauses, as in (7) and (8). It is followed by *to*, as in (11).

4. CANADA: inanimate, concrete, proper, count, non-human
   WINE: inanimate, concrete, common, mass, non-human
   MOUSE1: animate, concrete, common, count, non-human
   MOUSE2: inanimate, concrete, common, count, non-human
   TRUTH: abstract, common, mass
   RUMOUR: abstract, common, count

GLASS1: inanimate, concrete, mass, non-human
GLASS2: inanimate, concrete, count, non-human
GRANT1: inanimate, concrete, count, non-human
GRANT2: inanimate, concrete, mass, non-human

Chapter 6

1. 1. *Jane believes that the earrings she got from Susan are real silver*   Main Clause
       that the earrings she got from Susan are real silver   Complement Clause
       she got from Susan   Relative Clause
    2. *I'll believe it*   Main Clause
       when I see it   Adverbial Clause of Time
    3. *If you think Scotland are ever going to win the European Championship*   Adverbial Clause of Condition
       Scotland are ever going to win the European Championship   Complement Clause
       you must be a real optimist   Main Clause
    4. *The article in which the theory was put forward is now unobtainable*   Main Clause
       in which the theory was put forward   Relative Clause
    5. *That Helen is to marry the man she met on holiday has surprised all her friends*   Main Clause
       That Helen is to marry the man she met on holiday   Complement Clause
       she met on holiday   Relative Clause
    6. *Celia did not say that you could keep the book that you borrowed*   Main Clause
       that you could keep the book that you borrowed   Complement Clause
       that you borrowed   Relative Clause
    7. *Because you are flying non-stop*   Adverbial Clause of Reason
       you will probably have severe jet-lag   Main Clause
    8. *He promised that he would be here on time*   Main Clause
       that he would be here on time   Complement Clause
       though I find it difficult to rely on him   Adverbial Clause of Concession
    9. *The woman whose car you think you have dented is our MP*   Main Clause
       whose car you think you have dented   Relative Clause
       you have dented   Complement Clause

10. *That you don't like my home-made vodka I find difficult to believe*   Main Clause
    That you don't like my home-made vodka   Complement Clause
11. *Since you think you are ready to sit the test*   Adverbial Clause of Reason
    you are ready to sit the test   Complement Clause
    come along tomorrow   Main Clause
12. *That the club regained the trophy dismayed the teams that had better players*   Main Clause
    That the club regained the trophy   Complement Clause
    that had better players   Relative Clause

2. 1. *We regret that the plan is impracticable*   Main Clause
      that the plan is impracticable   Complement Clause
   2. *They accept the theory that the world is flat*   Main Clause
      that the world is flat   Complement Clause (modifying *theory*)
   3. *They accept the theory that the group proposed*   Main Clause
      that the group proposed   Relative Clause (modifying *theory*)
   4. *Did Fiona say who would be at the party?*   Main Clause
      who would be at the party   Complement Clause (modifying *say*)
   5. *Which of the candidates will be elected is quite unpredictable*   Main Clause
      Which of the candidates will be elected   Complement Clause (modifying *is unpredictable*)
   6. *It is believed by some historians that Napoleon was poisoned*   Main Clause
      that Napoleon was poisoned   Complement Clause (modifying *believed*)

3. 1. *Kirsty went out*
      (and) forgot to switch off the gas fire
      two conjoined main clauses
   2. *that she wrote several novels*
      and threw them away
      two conjoined complement clauses (modifying *know*)
   3. *who ignored the ban*
      and printed the story
      two conjoined relative clauses
   4. *If you go walking on the hills in winter*
      and do not take proper equipment
      two conjoined adverbial clauses of condition

4. 1. *They are pioneering a new geography in which they will establish when new races settled in particular regions*   Main Clause
in which they will establish when new races settled in particular regions   Relative Clause
when new races settled in particular regions   Complement Clause (modifying *establish*)

   2. *A geneticist says the Pacific islands are an ideal testing ground for the theory that the Pacific was colonised from west to east*   Main Clause
the Pacific islands are an ideal testing ground for the theory that the Pacific was colonised from west to east   Complement Clause (modifying *says*)
that the Pacific was colonised from west to east   Complement Clause (modifying *theory*)

   3. *The history begins with the day when the chief medical officer for Vanuatu noticed that a large number of people there suffered from anaemia*   Main Clause
when the chief medical officer for Vanuatu noticed that a large number of people there suffered from anaemia   Relative Clause (modifying *day*)
that a large number of people there suffered from anaemia   Complement Clause (modifying *noticed*)

   4. *He was advised to treat them with iron supplements*   Main Clause
so he contacted scientists at Oxford who found that half of the donors suffered from alpha-thalassaemia, which is usually linked to the presence of malaria   Adverbial Clause of Result/Consequence
who found that half of the donors suffered from alpha-thalassaemia, which is usually linked to the presence of malaria   Relative Clause (modifying *scientists*)
that half of the donors suffered from alpha-thalassaemia, which is usually linked to the presence of malaria   Complement Clause (modifying *found*)
which is usually linked to the presence of malaria   Relative Clause (modifying *alpha-thalassaemia*)

   5. *It seems that the gene protects against malaria*   Main Clause
since carriers of the alpha 3.7 mutant will not die of malaria even if they contract a severe bout   Adverbial Clause of Reason (modifying the Main Clause)
even if they contract a severe bout   Adverbial Clause of Condition (modifying the Adverbial Clause of Reason)

   6. *Although anthropological studies have been inconclusive*   Adverbial Clause of Concession
previous biological research has suggested that there was no contact while the Melanesians were moving east   Main Clause
that there was no contact while the Melanesians were moving east

Complement Clause (modifying *has suggested*)
while the Melanesians were moving east
Adverbial Clause of Time (modifying *that there was no contact*)

Chapter 7

1. 1. *to learn two languages simultaneously to a high level inside three months*
   infinitive; the understood subject is *she*
   2. *travelling to Glasgow by the M8 at this time of year*
   gerund; understood subject is *I*
   3. *Having looked at all the exercises very carefully*
   free participle; understood subject is *We*
   4. *Sheila quickly hiding something under the chair when I came in*
   gerund with an overt subject, *Sheila*
   5. *Imogen's being so keen to spend her holidays tramping tirelessly round art galleries*   gerund with an overt subject, *Imogen's*
   6. *With all the children coming home for Christmas and the New Year*
   gerund with an overt subject, *all the children*
   7. *His car sold*   free participle with an overt subject, *His car*

2. 1. WH, indirect word order
   2. WH, indirect word order
   3. WH, indirect word order
   4. yes–no, indirect (John's question is *Are you ready yet?*)
   5. WH, indirect
   6. WH, direct
   7. WH, direct word order
   8. WH, direct word order
   9. WH, direct word order
   10. WH, direct word order
   11. WH, direct word order
   12. WH, direct word order
   13. WH, direct word order
   14. WH, indirect word order + yes–no, direct word order
   15. WH indirect word order + yes–no, direct word order

Chapter 8

1. All the grammatical subjects are involved in person and number linkage with the verb. Other properties are mentioned as they occur.

   1. *Mr Weston*: grammatical and logical subject
   2. *Mr Woodhouse*: grammatical subject
   Mr Weston: logical subject

3. *Mr Weston*: grammatical and logical subject
4. *The other guests*: grammatical subject; no logical subject
5. *All the soldiers*: *all* moves to the right, as in (6); logical subject
6. *The soldiers*: grammatical and logical subject
7. *The young ladies* like all the soldiers
   the young ladies: grammatical and logical subject; *all* cannot move to the right, (8) is unacceptable and *the soldiers* is not the grammatical subject
8. *The young ladies*: grammatical and logical subject
9. *Mr Collins*: grammatical and logical subject: controls the interpretation of *himself*
10. *Mr D'Arcy*: grammatical and logical subject; understood subject of *to persuade*
11. *Mr D'Arcy*: grammatical and logical subject; pivot in the coordinate construction
12. *The oldest Bennet girls*: grammatical subject; no logical subject; *both* has moved to the right – compare *both the oldest Bennet girls*

2. 1. *with a hamper of food*: oblique object
   2. *us*: indirect object; *a single malt*: direct object
   3. *Alice*: indirect object; a meal: *direct object*
   4. *Caroline*: oblique object
   5. *Robin's work*: oblique object
   6. *Fiona*: indirect object; *her history of the department*: direct object
   7. *an e-mail message*: direct object; *Ronnie*: oblique object
   8. *the fire*: oblique object; *itself*: direct object
   9. *Who*: oblique object
   10. *the grass*: direct object (If = 'The dog tore the grass up')
       the grass: oblique object (If = 'The dog raced up the grass')

Chapter 9

1. Nouns have different suffixes (case endings) depending on which class they belong to. Compare *greg* + *em*, the direct object in (1), *carruc* + *am*, the direct object in (2), and *oppid* + *um*, the direct object in (6). Adjectives modifying direct objects take different suffixes depending on a given noun. Compare *magn* + *um* in (1), *magn* + *am* in (2) and *magn* + *um* in (6). In the COPULA construction, the adjective complementing *est* 'is' takes different suffixes depending on which class the subject noun belongs to: *parv* + *a* in (3), *magn* + *us* in (4) and *magn* + *um* in (5).

2. Main verbs have the -*s* suffix regardless of person and number. Where *do* and *have* are main verbs, the forms are *does* and *has*, as in (6), (7), (10).

Where *do* is an auxiliary verb. it takes the form *do*, as in (4), (8), (11), (14), (15), (16). *Have* takes the form *has* when it is a main verb, as in (7), and *have* when it is the auxiliary verb in the Perfect tense, as in (11). In (12), *has* expresses necessity; the form indicates that here it is a main verb.

Chapter 11

1. 1, 2   different in meaning
   3, 4   different in meaning
   5, 6   different in meaning, but note that the interpretation may be affected by a property of points – they are usually quite small and, no matter the syntax, the spray from a can may well cover them all.
   7, 8   different in meaning
   9, 10   no difference in meaning; *supply* does not have to do with covering a particular area.
   11, 12   no difference in meaning, thanks to the use of *cram* in both examples. *Cram* is appropriate only where a container is full or becomes full.
   13, 14   no difference in meaning
   15, 16   potentially different in meaning in context. Where two or three strips of bark are hanging off, the deer could be described as stripping the bark off the tree, but just these strips. Example (16) can only be used if the deer removed all the bark; that is, its action affected the entire tree.

2. Examples (1) and (4) are acceptable, (2) and (3) are not. *Pour* can only be applied to what is to be contained in a container, and *fill* can only be applied to the container.
   The standard analysis is that (5) and (8) are unacceptable but (6) and (7) are not. *Steal* is applied to whatever is removed from its owner, and *rob* is applied to the owner. Note that examples like (7) are becoming frequent in British English, at least in the spoken language.

3. *I*: Agent
   I recorded several versions of this story in Urfa is an answer to the question *What did you do?*
   versions: Patient
   story: Source (see comments below on *hill*)
   Urfa: Place
   Father Abraham: Patient
   Father Abraham was born ... is an answer to the question *What happened to Father Abraham?*
   cave: Place

citadel mount: Place
he: Patient
castellan: Source
Nimrod: Agent
cradle: Patient
pillars: Patient
acropolis: Place
catapult: Patient/Goal (the latter on the grounds that Nimrod moved the pillars into the set of catapults by his adaptation)
baby: Patient
furnace: Goal
bottom: Place
hill: Source (controversial, but there is a link in many Indo-European languages between possession and source)
Almighty: Agent
plan: Neutral
Mankind: Goal
danger: Place
furnace: Patient
pool: Goal
carp: Source (but also controversial. The carp are presented as the cause of the pool's being full, and in many languages Source and Cause are expressed in the same or very similar ways.)
carp: Agent (*caught the baby*)
baby: Patient
him: Patient
poolside: Goal
Abraham: Agent
anyone: Agent (anyone eating the carp)
who: Agent (in the Relative Clause *who ate the carp*)
carp: Patient

Chapter 12

1. 1. *may*: deontic, permission
   2. *may*: epistemic, possibility
   3. *might*: epistemic, possibility
   4. *might*: deontic, permission (but old-fashioned usage)
   5. *can*: deontic, permission
   6. *can*: epistemic, possibility
   7. *could*: epistemic, possibility
   8. *mustn't*: deontic, necessity

9. *mustn't*: epistemic, conclusion
10. *can't*: epistemic, conclusion
11. *must*: epistemic, conclusion
12. *must*: deontic, necessity

Chapter 13

1. (1a) entails (1b)
   (2a) does not entail (2b)
   (3a) entails (3b)
   (4a) does not entail (4b)
   (5a) entails (5b)
   (6a) entails (6b)
   (7a) does not entail (7b)
   (8a) entails (8b)

2. 1. non-stative
   2. stative
   3. stative
   4. non-stative
   5. stative
   6. non-stative
   7. stative
   8. stative
   9. stative
   10. non-stative

3. 1a acceptable; appropriate if 'she' has declared an intention to carry out the action
   1b acceptable, but sounds more like a prediction
   2a acceptable; equivalent to 'Would you like me to shut the window?'
   2b acceptable, but sounds as if the speaker is asking the hearer if he/she can guess what the speaker is going to do
   3a acceptable, request
   3b not fully acceptable, request
   3c Acceptability increased by deletion of *please*. Sounds more like a question about the hearer's intention.
   4a acceptable
   4b unacceptable
   5a acceptable, prediction
   5b unacceptable, a statement about someone's intention, which makes *I suppose* seem out of place

Further reading

This section indicates books on syntax in general and the syntax of English that are within the range of anyone who has read this introduction and worked through at least some of the exercises. The items mentioned below are intermediate in level, and are not necessarily whole books but also chapters from books. Since generative grammar is not covered here, the items on that topic are introductory and not intermediate.

General

Hurford, James R. (1994), *Grammar: A Student's Guide*, Cambridge: Cambridge University Press.

This is not a textbook but is organised in the form of a dictionary-encyclopaedia. The entries are excellent and cover the central concepts used in grammatical descriptions. It focuses on English.

Tallerman, Maggie (1998), *Understanding Syntax*, London: Arnold.

Tallerman's book and this one overlap, but Tallerman introduces data from many different languages. There are exercises without answers, but an e-mail help address is given.

Crystal, David (1995), *Cambridge Encyclopaedia of the English Language*, Cambridge: Cambridge University Press.

Like Hurford's book, this is not a textbook but an encyclopaedia to be dipped into. It is full of information about all areas of English and the usage of English, and the text is clear and lively, with splendid examples and many fascinating illustrations. Just the book for language enthusiasts on a dull winter day (or any other day for that matter).

English grammar

Biber, Douglas, Stig Johansson, Geoffrey Leech, Susan Conrad and Edward Finegan (1999), *Longman Grammar of Spoken and Written English*, London: Longman.

Quirk, Randolph and Sidney Greenbaum (1973), *A University Grammar of English*, London: Longman.
Quirk, Randolph, Sidney Greenbaum, Geoffrey Leech and Jan Svartvik (1985), *A Comprehensive Grammar of the English Language*, London: Longman.

The above three books are not textbooks for reading but grammars to be dipped into. They are for the reader interested in investigating specific points of English grammar.

Constituent structure and dependency relations

Fabb, Nigel (1994), *Sentence Structure*, London: Routledge.

A very straightforward and concise account with data from English and other languages. Exercises but without answers.

Thomas, Linda (1993), *Beginning Syntax*, Oxford: Blackwell.

A clear account of constituent structure, focusing on English, that goes well beyond Chapters 1, 2 and 10 here. Many exercises with answers.

Clauses

Most theoretical discussion of clauses takes place in the context of generative grammar, where clauses and sentences are not usually clearly distinguished. The most accessible discussions of subordinate clauses (of English) are still to be found in the grammars by Quirk et al. referred to above.

Grammar and semantics

Blake, Barry (1994), *Case*, Cambridge: Cambridge University Press.

Chapters 1, 2.1–2.2 and 3 give a good introduction.

Frawley, William (1992), *Linguistic Semantics*, Hillsdale, NJ and Hove/London: Lawrence Erlbaum Associates.

Chapter 7 on aspect and Chapter 8 on tense offer a more detailed discussion than in Chapter 13 here.

Givon, Talmy (1984), *Syntax: A functional-typological introduction*, vol. 1, Amsterdam: John Benjamin, chapter 8.

This book is long in the tooth by some standards, but the discussion of tense and aspect is accessible and well worth reading. There is a good range of interesting data.

Goddard, Cliff (1998), *Semantic Analysis: A Practical Introduction*, Oxford: Oxford University Press.

Chapter 11, 'Grammatical Categories', covers topics not dealt with here, namely pronouns, classifiers and Experiencer constructions and uses data from non-Indo-European languages. Chapter 10 on causatives is also well worth reading.

Palmer, Frank (1986), *Mood and Modality*, Cambridge: Cambridge University Press.

Chapter 1 gives a good overview of the topic. Readers who enjoy the section on mood in Chapter 12 here could take on Palmer's chapter 2 on epistemic modality and chapter 3 on deontic modality.

Generative grammar

Haegeman, Liliane (1991), *Introduction to Government and Binding Theory*, Oxford: Blackwell.

Haegeman's book describes a model of generative grammar that is not the latest. However, it describes the essentials of Chomskyan generative grammar very lucidly, in digestible portions and with many diagrams. From this book, anyone interested in generative grammar can proceed to more advanced treatments.

Index